MW00806841

BLACK
YELLOWDOGS

The Most Dangerous Citizen
Is Not Armed, But Uninformed

BEN KINCHLOW

NEW YORK

BLACK YELLOWDOGS
The Most Dangerous Citizen Is Not Armed, But Uninformed

© 2008 Ben Kinchlow. All rights reserved.

No part of this publication may be reproduced or transmitted in any form or by any means, mechanical or electronic, including photocopying and recording, or by any information storage and retrieval system, without permission in writing from author or publisher (except by a reviewer, who may quote brief passages and/or show brief video clips in a review).

Library of Congress Control Number: 007935677

ISBN: 978-1-60037-285-8 (Hardcover)

ISBN: 978-1-60037-284-1 (Paperback)

Published by:

MORGAN · JAMES   Kids Against Hunger™
THE ENTREPRENEURIAL PUBLISHER™   *The Starvation Solution*

Morgan James Publishing, LLC
1225 Franklin Ave Ste 325
Garden City, NY 11530-1693
Toll Free 800-485-4943
www.MorganJamesPublishing.com

Cover by:	**Interior Design by:**
Sean Kinchlow	Tony Laidig
www.seankinchlow.com	www.thecoverexpert.com
sk@seankinchlow.com	tony@thecoverexpert.com

TABLE OF CONTENTS

FREE $50 BONUS OFFER!

Free Audio Recording

by

Ben Kinchlow

"THE REAL AMERICA"

African-American History

In this two-CD set, Ben Kinchlow and renowned historian David Barton reveal little known, and often shocking, information about African-American history. Knowledge is power and freedom, and the most dangerous citizen is not armed, but uninformed.

Register your copy of *Black YellowDogs* today at:

www.blackyellowdogs.com

No additional purchase is required.

INTRODUCTION

The following are all black on the outside, white on the inside:

Oreo; Bounty Bar; Coconut; Tom; Uncle Tom; Boot-Licking Uncle Tom; Official Government Issue Uncle Tom; Fried Chicken/Biscuit Eating Uncle Tom; House Nigger; Boy; Foot Shuffling Steppin' Fetchit; Handkerchief Head; Trojan Horse; Anti-Black-Pro-White; Sambo; Sell Out; Neutralized Negro; Unauthentic Black; De-Blacked; Fraud; Con Man; Ventriloquist Dummy; Right-Wing Conspirator; White Wannabe; Clarence, (as in Thomas); Non-Practicing Black; Zebra; Black Republican; Reverend Pork Chop; Judas.

I have provided the foregoing ready reference list of descriptive phrases for my critics, those nattering nabobs of negativity, and defenders of the arbitrarily established politically correct "Black Position." The preceding are but a sampling of the more polite titles reserved for use on those Blacks who fail to toe the party line. Let the record show, I have already been called all, or most all, of the above (including some I choose not to dignify by repeating).

YELLOW DOGS COME IN ALL COLORS

She was a mother, a Baptist, a Democrat, a White, and from the South (in that order) sending her son into the world via the military. "Son," she admonished him sternly, "be a good boy and always remember - we are Baptists and Democrats." Having been raised a Baptist, he had some idea what Baptists do, but precious little information as to how one should conduct oneself as a *Democrat*. "Mama?" he asked, wanting to please and bring honor to the family, "what does it mean to be a Democrat?" "Well, son," she paused, "it means... er, ah, ahem"... finally, in a fit of frustration, she gave him the definition he still remembers some 50 years later: "Hell, what damned difference does it make? We believe it anyway!" Apparently, he never did find out, or maybe he did. At any rate, he grew up to become a Presbyterian and a Republican.

WHO YOU CALLIN' A YELLOW DOG?

In the 1928 presidential elections, senior Senator Tom Heflin (D-AL) decided not to support New York Governor Al Smith, the Democrat candidate for president. He chose instead, the Republican, Herbert Hoover. Hard-line rank and file Southern Democrats were outraged. Despite the fact that this was Alabama (they were Deep South Protestants and he was Catholic, and a Yankee to boot), dogged party loyalists were determined to support Smith. When asked why, the leader of the hardliners replied, *"I'd vote for a yellow dog if he ran on the Democratic ticket."* The press popularized the phrase *"I'd vote for a yellow dog..."* and subsequently, the phrase "Yellow Dog Democrat" has become a part of the American political lexicon. A "Yellow Dog Democrat" is traditionally someone who votes Democrat, period, no matter the issue or candidate. As a black American who consistently voted Democrat (when I did vote), I easily qualified as a "Black Yellow Dog." Unfortunately, many black Americans have, as did I, engaged in a deadly game of "follow the leader."

Made aware of certain historical facts, I began to challenge the flawed concept of voting in blind faith for any party or candidate. Tragically, it seems we have ignored an ancient warning that could easily be applied to many of our African-American leaders: *"Beware... they are blind guides. And if the blind guide the blind, both shall fall into a pit."* It is my fond hope that these are, indeed, merely blind guides, for I shudder to consider the alternative. Additional fuel will, no doubt, be added by this quote from Justice Clarence Thomas:

> *"I have come.... to assert my right to think for myself, to refuse to have my ideas assigned to me, as though I was an intellectual slave."* [1] (Couldn't have said it better myself, Your Honor)

Born in a small Texas town at the close of the Great Depression to a hardworking laborer and his schoolteacher wife, I know first hand about biscuits and fried chicken (we raised chickens and rolled out biscuits) and I have hands-on experience with *doin' without* and *hand me downs*. Blacks knew "Jim Crow" intimately. Black kids learned early on about lynchings and how to avoid putting oneself in a potential *situation* and we discussed them when they happened. In the wild, this would have been tantamount to learning survival skills.

In a four-classes-in-one-room, two-room "separate but equal" school, we learned reading, writing, and *arithmetic* ~ "No Ben, it is not *'rithmatic."* We also learned discipline and respect for our elders. Every "yes" or "no" to an adult had a "Sir" or "Ma'am" attached to it and all adults came with "Mr." or "Mrs." in front of their name. *Mrs.* Harris taught 1st through 4th grade in Room 1, and *Mrs.* Jewel (first name, because she was younger) taught 5th through 8th grade in Room 2. Four different grades in the same room, at the same time, all taught by one teacher left no time for youthful exuberance. Recess was for play. Classrooms were for learning. There was little time for individual tutoring. Mama (my 5th through 8th grade teacher) had maxims. One Mama maxim was, *"Find things out for yourself. That's what books are for. Form the habit of reading and you can know."* There was once an old joke about books and black people: *"When the white man wants to keep something hidden from black folks, he puts it in a book. He knows the Negro ain't gonna' pick up no book."* (Mama didn't think that was funny.)

Black children were not taught that we were objects of pity, disadvantaged, or underprivileged. We learned the hard facts about slavery from "old folks" and our family histories; some of us had great-grandparents who had been born in slavery. My great-grandfather, Ben Kinchlow, was born a slave.

Everybody in the black community *knew* who the "ne'r do wells," "loose" women, and "worthless" men were. Ask any successful black entrepreneur or business owner over fifty and you'll find we got precious little support from our elders for any concept of being deprived by virtue of being black. Slavery was not an excuse or justification for failure. Back then, black folks' version of affirmative action was "root hog or die." My mother, Mrs. Jewel Kinchlow, earned a M.Ed. from Huston-Tillotson, a historically black college in Austin, Texas. Mama, like thousands of other *disadvantaged* young Blacks, worked her way through college, graduated, went to work, and attended summer school to earn her Master's Degree. (The original purpose of the HBCU - Historically Black Colleges and Universities - was to provide Blacks the educational opportunities denied by HWCUs - Historically White Colleges and Universities. Often times we have not taken advantage of educational opportunities and much of whatever else we may or may not have done should not be blamed on the system.) No one ever taught, thought, or believed we were the government's responsibility. "Relief" (aka modern welfare), spoken of in whispers ("not in front of the children") was not a *right,* it was a disgrace, and to be "gotten off of" as soon as humanly possible. Black pride wasn't about Afros, dashikis (African clothing), and boys wearing braids. It was about the girl who didn't get pregnant out of wedlock, but finished school, and the boy who got a degree or a steady job and supported the girl he had *married,* not gotten pregnant and abandoned.

Let me be perfectly clear ~ Blacks are not born wards of the state. Our mental capacities are not underdeveloped because of something that happened to our ancestors over 200 years ago. Tens of millions of words and countless scholarly works have been written about the "Black," "Negro," "Afro," and now "African-American" experience or condition, before, during, and after what few intelligent people would deny was an egregious stain on the fabric of the American experiment...slavery. This small work should not be misconstrued as exhaustive in any sense of the term. It is merely one man's attempt, as Justice Thomas suggested, "to refuse to have my ideas assigned to me."

Following Mama's advice, I formed the reading habit, and I have been shocked, dismayed, enlightened, and encouraged by what I've read. I challenge all who may disagree with what they read here to research the historical facts, arrive at your own conclusions, and don't let me or anyone else make decisions for you.

Think for yourself.

(By the way, I didn't put this stuff in a book to hide it from black folks. I didn't think that joke was funny either.)

CHAPTER 1

BLACK SLAVE MASTERS?

AS IT WAS IN THE BEGINNING

The first Africans to arrive at Jamestown, Virginia were not slaves, but <u>indentured servants</u>, having specified periods of servitude. Indentured servants were not slaves. This distinction is critical. In 1619, indentured servants, white or black, received precisely the same treatment. At the conclusion of their period of servitude, each was entitled to freedom, citizenship, and a land grant of fifty acres. Throughout the colonial period, the basis of land disposition was *grants*, as all land was held in trust for the King and dispensed by the local government in accordance with his wishes. Land grants in Virginia were issued in accordance with a "headrights" system. Under this system, every person who paid his own way to Virginia would be entitled to fifty acres of land - a headright.

Many Englishmen *indentured* themselves for a period of years, usually seven or less, in exchange for passage to the new world. A father could sell (indenture) a family of four and, all things being equal, qualify for a parcel of 200 acres. At the conclusion of the period of servitude, each family member was granted title to fifty acres, given their freedom, and subsequently enjoyed all the rights and privileges of other citizens in the community. There was no stigma attached.

There were both economic benefits and civic challenges associated with this practice ~ British law protected the rights of the individual; the master's power over his indentured servants was limited; and a specific skill must be taught. However, *white* indentureds could (and often did) slip off to a new colony. A permanent solution had to be found. One was; the Virginia Company changed the rules to allow anyone to pay any person's transportation to the colony in exchange for a period of indentured servitude. The knowledge of a skill of any kind was not included in this contract. Whoever paid the cost would receive fifty acres of land for each passage purchased. This gave wealthy businessmen the ability to import new workers and negotiate the right to claim the fifty acres. Bonded servants would now get nothing but a trip and often found themselves without rights or freedom. As white indentured servant Thomas Best wrote from Virginia in 1623, *"My master Atkins hath sold me for 150 pounds sterling like a damned slave."* [1]

How did this state of affairs come about? How could people who came here to escape bondage institutionalize it?

BLIND PEOPLE HAVE ONE ADVANTAGE - THEY CAN'T SEE UGLY

Jamestown, Virginia: August 1619 - Into Chesapeake Bay sailed a vessel ~ *"...a Dutch man-of-warre that sold us twenty Negars."* ~ John Rolf, Virginia tobacco farmer

That these Blacks were indentured servants, not slaves, is supported by an entry in the same diary that referenced their arrival:

> "...*Young maids* [90 white females] *to make wives for so many of the former tenants* [colonists]" were priced by the Virginia Company at not less than "*one hundredth and fiftie [pounds] of the best leafe Tobacco.*" [2]

Thus began what has become arguably one of the most intriguing relationships of the past two centuries.

According to British law, every *Christian* was equal before the law at that time. Judgment was based not on race, but upon being Christian or non-Christian. Blacks, if they became Christian and were baptized, were allowed, as were other British citizens, to earn their freedom. These *bound servants* - black or white; male or female - were considered simply a source of cheap labor, and once the term was served no stigma remained.

Here, history takes a bizarre turn. When I came upon this one particularly astonishing bit of information, I was flabbergasted. Not once had I ever heard so much as a whisper of this, and it flew in the face of everything I *knew - everybody knew -* about the origins of slavery in the English colonies. Talk about political incorrectness!

Using the method of claiming the fifty acres of an indentured servant, one colonist, Anthony Johnson, by indenturing his own family members, was able to secure 250 acres of land. His sons, by the same strategy, gained an additional 650 acres. The Johnsons settled on "Pungoteague Creek" on the Eastern Shore of Virginia and thrived for almost forty years. Johnson raised livestock, prospered, and as was customary with prosperous landowners, indentured one black and several white servants. He sued in court and won several cases, but one case in particular would set the stage for a dramatic shift in the work force, indelibly change the American landscape, and impact relationships between Blacks and Whites for centuries.

There are several reports as to the origin of this landmark case. One report says John Casor, the black indentured servant, "swindled" Johnson out of the remainder of his servitude; another says he "convinced" a white neighbor, Robert Parker, that he was being illegally detained; and still another says the family convinced Johnson to free Casor. Whatever the reason, Johnson was not satisfied with the result and took Casor and Parker to court, alleging that Casor had not been purchased as a servant, but as a slave. Understand the true significance of this case - Johnson did not sue to have John Casor fulfill some measure of a debt of servitude. Instead, he insisted the court grant his petition *"hee had ye Negro for his life."* He was claiming the services of John Casor for the remainder of Casor's natural life. To my knowledge, there is no earlier record of judicial support given to slavery in Virginia *except* as a punishment for crime. Anthony Johnson was asking the court to award him John Casor (who had committed no crime) as a *slave*. Though Parker and one other influential landowner, both white, sided with Casor, the court ruled for Johnson.

Quoted in the original language taken from the original documents is the decision of County Court:

Court of Northampton; Eight Mar, Anno 1654 ...

Whereas complaint was this daye made to ye court by ye humble peticion of Anth. Johnson Negro ag[ains]t Mr. Robert Parker that hee detayneth one John Casor a Negro the plaintiffs Serv[an]t under pretense yt the sd Jno. Casor a Negro is a free-man the court seriously considering & maturely weighing ye premises doe fynd that ye sd Mr. Reboert Parker most unrightly keepeth ye sd Negro John Casor from his r[igh]t of mayster Anth. Johnson as it appeareth by ye Deposition of Capt. Samll Gold smith & many probable circumstances. be it therefore ye Judge-ment of ye court & ordered that ye sd Jno. Casor negro, shall forthwith bee turned into ye service of his sd master Anthony Johnson and that the sd Mr. Robert Parker make payment of all charges in the suite and execution.[3]

Hold on! What was that?! To grasp the significance of what I'd just read, I needed to read it slowly and in modern English:

"Whereas complaint was this day made to the court by the humble petition of Anthony Johnson, Negro, against Mr. Robert Parker that he detains one John Casor, a Negro, the plaintiff's servant under pretense that the said John Casor is a freeman. The court seriously considering and maturely weighing the premises do find that the said Mr. Robert Park-er most unrightly keeps the said Negro John Casor from his rightful master Anthony Johnson, as it appears by the Deposi-tion of Capt. Samuel Goldsmith and many probable circum-stances. Be it therefore the Judgment of the court and ordered that said John Casor Negro, shall forthwith be turned into the service of his said master, Anthony Johnson, and that the said Mr. Robert Parker make payment of all charges in the suit and execution." (Eighth March, Year 1654)

This is apparently the first legal sanction of slavery (not for a crime) in the New World. From evidence found in the earliest legal documents, Anthony Johnson must be recognized as the nation's first official legal slaveholder. Johnson had been captured in Angola and brought to America as an indentured servant, and herein is the bizarre turn. Anthony Johnson was a black man.

The father of legalized slavery in America was a Black man!

Whoa! I'm thinking to myself - this cannot be! How could a "brother" do that to a "bro?!" How could a black man take away the freedom of another black man? I was disoriented, off balance. After all, I *knew*, *everybody knew*, "Whitey" had been the one who chained us. And now I discover the first slave owner was a *black man* - and the first anti-slavery protest came from a *white man?!* Surely, this was an aberration. Black people could not possibly possess the *inhuman* traits of the "white monsters." Blacks would surely not enslave their own people. No way! Could I be wrong about this? Naaah! But even if it *were* true, there just could not be *another one*. Johnson may have been the first, but he was most surely the *only* one! The danger of knowledge is its tendency to unsettle. Someone said, "Knowledge is power." Someone much wiser said, *"With much knowledge is much sorrow."*

This from a 1795 court document from Henrico County, Virginia:

> *"Know all men by these presents that I, James Radford of the County of Henrico for and in consideration of the sum of thirty-three pounds current money of Virginia to me in hand paid by George Radford **a black freeman** of the city of Richmond hath bargained and sold unto George Radford one negro woman [A]ggy, to have and to hold the said negro slave*

*[A]ggy unto the said George Radford his heirs and assigns for-
ever."* [4] (emphasis added)

Black slave masters? Wouldn't a black slave master be head-
line news? Some scholars, like John H. Russell, PhD, a professor
of political science at Whitman College, Walla Walla, Washington, believe that in those days "free Blacks owning black slaves
was so common as to pass unnoticed, except in the case of
court records." He cites: "Deeds of sale and transfer of slaves to
free Negroes, wills of free Negroes providing for a future disposition of slaves, and records of suits for freedom against free
Negroes..." as ample evidence that Blacks owning Blacks was a
relatively common occurrence. And it didn't stop there. Black
slave masters did not die out in colonial times; the practice did
not end with the Johnsons, as the 1830 Census indicates.

THE OFFICIAL US CENSUS OF 1830

3,775 free Negroes owned 12,740 Negro slaves

Of the 10,689 free Blacks who lived in New Orleans in 1830,
more than 3,000 were slave masters. Almost 30% of the free
blacks in that city owned slaves. These mulattoes, quadroons,
and octoroons ~ mixed race, light skinned Negroes ~ owned
and, in some cases, rented their black slaves to Whites.

William Johnson, perhaps Mississippi's best known free
Black, was a slaveholder. In 1834, this Adams County native
owned roughly 3,000 acres in real property. He speculated in
farmland, rented real estate, owned a bathhouse, a delivery
firm, a toyshop, and he rented out his slaves.[5]

How could this be!? *White people* owned slaves. Everybody knows that only white people owned black people! Apparently not. Several free black slave masters in South Carolina owned as many as 30 or more slaves. Two other free Blacks owned a plantation and 170 slaves between the two of them!

The U.S. census report of 1860 showed almost 27 million Whites in the country, and *fewer than 385,000 individuals reported owning slaves*. That is about 1.4 percent of the total white population. Those who did have slaves reported owning five or less. Only the top one percent of the population owned fifty or more slaves.

To put this in perspective, eight million Whites lived in the slave states, and the average white male earned less than $4,000 per year. In the period between 1825 and 1830, the average price for young adult male slaves in Virginia was $400. One planter sold four slaves (gender unspecified) in 1826-1827 for $700, $600, $500, and $450. By early 1850, male slaves were advertised at $825 each, and females were priced at $700 and $600. By early 1861, with a civil war looming, prices for Virginia field hands had climbed to an average of $1,200 each. Prices were correspondingly high during the early months of 1861, when field hands were advertised from $1,600 to $1,650.[6] Slaves were expensive.

According to this same 1860 census, 261,988 southern Blacks were *not* slaves. One wealthy black sugar planter owned over 100 black slaves and had land holdings valued at over a quarter of a million dollars, making him one of the richest blacks in Louisiana, perhaps one of the richest Blacks in the United States. A widow and her son (black) owned a plantation and worked more than 150 slaves. This same census lists several Blacks owning 65 or more slaves. Blacks in one South Carolina city claimed over $1.5 million in taxable property, including slaves valued in excess of $300,000.

Since light-skinned Blacks owned dark-skinned Blacks, do lighter-skinned Blacks owe damages to darker-skinned Blacks? Can anyone say, "Rep-a-ra-tions?" *Brothers* were doing *brothers* in back then just as *brothers* are doing *brothers* in now. I am certain that some of my *brothers* will attempt to do me in with vitriolic disdain for this *feeble attempt to get the white man off the hook* by blaming our slavery on ourselves with *"Well, Blacks did it too!"*

Lest I be misinterpreted; the above information is in no way to be misconstrued as justification of institutionalized slavery. I offer this merely as evidence that injustice is, as justice should be, colorblind.

BLACK YELLOW DOGS

CHAPTER 2

USA! USA!

"*The right worship of God, according to the Simplicitie of the Gospell without the admixture of men's inventions,*" as outlined in the Mayflower Compact, brought the Pilgrims to America. This "right worship" repudiated the divine right of kings based on the Scriptural equality of all men. In 1776, the Declaration of Independence declared, "All men are created equal." The Biblical injunction "*Do unto others…*" and this Declaration contrasted jarringly with the practice of slavery in America.

Later, slavery would become an issue not easily dismissed. While most of the colonists opposed slavery on religious and moral grounds, Britain, for economic reasons, had consistently vetoed all efforts to abolish the practice. In the original draft of the Declaration of Independence there were 31 charges leveled against "*the present King of Great Britain,*" among them "*… imposing taxes on us without our consent.*" The familiar phrase "taxation without representation" leads many to the mistaken conclusion that the Revolutionary War was solely about taxes. There was almost universal support for abolishing taxes ~ but not slavery. Something as elemental and mundane as <u>survival</u> kept slavery from also being adopted as an issue in the New World. These thirteen small struggling colonies, previously operating as independent entities, had declared their independence from what was certainly one of the most powerful empires in existence at the time. It was imperative that they grasp every possible lifeline to survive, as success was by no means assured. For young America, it was life or death. As Benjamin Franklin said on July 4, 1776, *"We must all hang together, or assuredly we shall all hang separately."* [1]

It is a grievous error for TV pundits, ivory towered intellectuals, and "civil rights leaders" in custom made suits to judge the Founding Fathers in the glare of the neon lights of the 21st century. These were not simply hypocritical old white men, living luxuriously off slave labor. These men were patriots and they were also realists. Keep in mind, slavery was legal and flourished throughout most of the known world. Arab Muslims enslaved Christians, regardless of race; Europeans enslaved other Europeans; and China was probably the greatest merchant of human beings known to mankind. Abolishing slavery was an anomaly. This small struggling entity called "The United States of America" *must* survive. To lose the fledgling nation was to lose all *"...our lives, our fortunes, and our sacred honor."*

When and if American history is taught, it is usually the revisionist version, where America is portrayed as a villain on the world stage and any injustices (real and imagined) on the part of the early settlers are emphasized. The Founding Fathers are no longer portrayed as patriots and heroes, trusting in "Divine

Providence" and sacrificing all for liberty, but are regularly depicted as bigots, rakes, and hypocrites. Since American history is no longer a required subject in many of our high schools and institutions of higher learning, two seemingly prophetic statements have become a modern reality. Abigail Adams, wife of John Adams, said… *"Posterity, who are to reap the blessings, will scarcely be able to conceive the hardships and sufferings of their ancestors."*[2] Their son, John Quincy Adams, sixth president of the United States, perhaps paraphrasing his mother, said, *"Posterity… you will never know how much it has cost my generation to preserve your freedom. I hope you will make good use of it."* [3]

On July 4, 1776, the colonies declared independence from Britain and the United States of America was officially born. Britain would not take this treason lightly. Troops were dispatched to quell the "rebellion." A group of Redcoats landed in Boston, confronted some American patriots, and shots were fired. The first American casualty in what would become a desperate war for independence, fell, mortally wounded. Many have heard of "the shot heard around the world," but not whom it killed. It was no mere bystander or passerby, but a patriot, a revolutionary, a member of The Sons of Liberty, a dedicated group that included, among others, Paul Revere. The "shot heard around the world" killed Crispus Attucks, a free Black.

In the northern colonies, Blacks were citizens in every sense of the word. They were artisans, merchants, and ministers, and they were much aware of Britain's support of slavery. Britain made offers of freedom to slaves who would fight against the colonists, but many Blacks knew that any British offer of freedom was purely a political gesture designed to undermine the rebellion.

USA! USA!

As one of the most unique man-made documents in history, the Declaration of Independence contains some of the most powerful and inspirational truths known to man. It also includes a measure of political expediency. In the colonies, slavers did operate, but revisionist historians and left-leaning professors fail to note that the vast majority of the Founders abhorred slavery. Revisionist historians, intent on *unmasking* and *demythologizing* the Founding Fathers, fail to make mention of two specific references to slavery in Jefferson's *original* draft of the document:

> *"He [the King] has waged cruel war against human nature itself, violating its most sacred rights of life and liberty and the persons of a distant people, who never offended him, captivating and carrying them into slavery in another hemisphere, or to incur miserable death in their transportation thither. This piratical warfare, the opprobrium* [shameful conduct] *of infidel powers, is the warfare of the Christian king of Great Britain.*
>
> *Determined to keep open a market where men should be bought and sold... he is now exciting those very people to rise in arms among us, and to purchase that liberty of which he has deprived them, by murdering the people* [colonists] *upon whom he also obtruded them* [thrust slaves upon them]*..."* [4]

The southern colonies vehemently opposed the anti-slavery language. Their failure to participate in the Revolution would have sounded the death knell of the fledgling American dream. The offending paragraphs were subsequently dropped and the Declaration of Independence was adopted. The Constitution would later address the slave issue.

EXTRA! EXTRA! KING GEORGE AND SLAVERY KICKED OUT!

This bears repeating ~ the majority of the inhabitants of the northern colonies rejected the idea of slavery. It was in 1777, immediately after the signing of the Declaration of Independence, that Vermont, for example, amended its Constitution to ban slavery. Pennsylvania, Massachusetts, New Hampshire, Connecticut, Rhode Island, New York, and New Jersey immediately adopted anti-slavery legislation, freed their slaves, and banned the institution.

George Washington and other leading Founders such as Thomas Jefferson, John Adams, and Benjamin Rush believed that slavery was totally inconsistent with the principles fought for in the American Revolution. During the Revolution, Washington favored the idea of enlisting slaves in the war with the agreement that they would be freed upon discharge. He wrote, *"I can only say there is not a man living who wishes more sincerely than I do, to see a plan adopted for the abolition of it."* Since slavery was still legal in Virginia when he left the presidency, he secretly freed several of his slaves by leaving them behind at the end of his term. Washington's Last Will and Testament ordered freedom for all his slaves and commanded his heirs to clothe and feed those slaves who were "incapable of supporting themselves due to age or infirmity." His estate continued to fulfill this responsibility for over three decades after his death.

The slavery issue also dogged the Continental Congress. At the Constitutional Convention in Philadelphia in 1787, much of the debate centered on whether or not the delegates should immediately ban the importation of African slaves. South Carolina and Georgia delegates threatened to withdraw if the ban was put in place; those colonies would not join the new United States of America. The survival of the new Union was so endangered that concessions were granted allowing the African slave trade to continue until 1807.

In 1787, Congress banned slavery in the Midwest Territory while narrowly defeating Thomas Jefferson's earlier proposal to ban slavery in the Alabama and Mississippi territories. The Northwest Ordinance prohibited slavery in the Northwest Territory and this ordinance, along with existing state emancipation laws, created, for all intents and purposes, a free North. This territory became the states of Ohio, Indiana, Illinois, Michigan, and Wisconsin, all potential slave states except for the Three-Fifths Clause.

THREE-FIFTHS OF A REASON?

Probably one of the best-known, yet least understood, acts of the Founders is the *Three-Fifths Clause*. As recently as the 2000 Presidential election, this clause continued to be misinterpreted. At the Democrats' Shadow Convention in August, 2000, held in Los Angeles, "civil rights leader" Jesse Jackson declared: *"There was a lot of talk a few weeks ago* [at the Republican National Convention in Philadelphia] *about the Constitutional Convention in Philadelphia. In that Constitution, African-Americans were considered three-fifths of a human being."* [5]

Many tenured liberal professors, revisionist historians, and modern civil rights leaders (with an axe to grind?) depict the Founders as hypocrites at best, and racists at worst (or both). "The Founding Fathers," they confidently assert, "speak of 'all men created equal...' while they make Black people three-fifths of a person." The Three-Fifths Clause is then introduced as "evidence" of this duplicity. Let us take a brief, but objective, look at this "duplicitous" act.

THE CONSTITUTION OF THE UNITED STATES

<u>Article I; Section 2; Clause 3</u>:

<u>Representatives</u> <u>and</u> <u>direct</u> <u>Taxes</u> <u>shall</u> <u>be</u> <u>apportioned</u>...among the several States, which may be included within this Union, <u>according</u> <u>to</u> <u>their</u> <u>respective</u> <u>Numbers</u>, which shall be determined by adding to the whole Number of free Persons, including those bound to Service for a Term of Years, and excluding Indians not taxed, <u>three fifths of all other Persons</u>. (emphasis added)

I call your attention first to the underlined portions: <u>*Representatives and direct Taxes shall be apportioned...according to their respective Numbers*</u>. The population of a state determines the number of representatives that state has in Congress. At the time of the Constitutional Convention, it was one representative for every thirty thousand counted. "In 1776, slaves comprised *40%* of the population of the colonies from Maryland south to Georgia, but well below *10%* in the colonies to the North." [6]

The southern states wanted slaves counted for the purpose of representation. The northern contingent was quite willing to count the slaves provided they were:

1) Given their freedom

2) Given the right to vote

The South was adamant; there would be no such conditions! Slaves were *property*! The northern delegates countered, "We shall count our horse and cattle for representative purposes!" Founder Elbridge Gerry from Massachusetts wondered, *"Why then should the Blacks, who were property in the South, be in the rule of representation more than the cattle and horses of the North?"* [7] Free Blacks voted in the North but not the South. Founder James Wilson of Pennsylvania, agreed with Gerry: *"Are they [slaves] admitted as citizens? Then why are they not admitted on an equality with white citizens? Are they [slaves] admitted as property? Then why is not other property admitted into computation?"* [8]

The northern delegates insisted that they were perfectly willing to count slaves, provided they were freed and permitted to vote. The southern delegates were threatening to walk out and according to records the Constitutional Convention was on the verge of a collapse. After much rancorous debate, Mr. Wilson, a signer of both the Declaration and the Constitution, finally offered a compromise that proved acceptable to the majority. He proposed to <u>count every five slaves as three</u>, *<u>thus "three fifths" (60%) of the slave population would be counted for representational purposes</u>*. It was a compromise, though not a perfect solution, and many in the North saw it as unfair. The Massachusetts legislature immediately passed a resolution objecting to the Three-Fifths Clause because "a planter in Georgia possessing fifty slaves may be considered as having thirty votes, while a farmer of Massachusetts, having equal or greater property, is confined to a single vote."

The Three-Fifths Clause was clearly designed to limit the political power and legislative influence of the slave states. It had absolutely nothing to do with the value of a human being, and to infer otherwise is ignorance at best or, at worst, blatant hypocrisy. Not to single out Rev. Jackson, but as he and numerous other critics of the Three-Fifths Clause (black and white) are both intelligent and educated, one can hardly ascribe ignorance. Dare one infer motive? But of course, civil rights "leaders" are not needed if civil rights have been realized.

Frederick Douglass, who escaped from slavery some seventy years later, initially believed that the Constitution was pro-slavery.

> "... Brought directly, when I escaped from slavery, into contact with a class of abolitionists regarding the Constitution as a slaveholding instrument...it is not strange that I assumed the Constitution to be just what their interpretation made it." [9]

> "My new circumstances compelled me to re-think the whole subject, and to study, with some care... By such a course of thought and reading, I was conducted to the conclusion that the Constitution of the United States...not only contained no guarantees in favor of slavery, but, on the contrary, was in its letter and spirit an anti-slavery instrument." [10]

We owe it to ourselves and our progeny to do no less than Frederick Douglass who, based on his own study, concluded that the Constitution was, in fact, an anti-slavery document.

Thomas Jefferson is constantly referenced to support the charges of hypocrisy leveled at the Founders by the leftist contingent that, interestingly enough, overwhelmingly vote Democrat; the facts, however, contradict their claims. Though Jefferson did own slaves, he authored the first attempt to end slavery and, in fact, introduced a law in 1784 in the Continental Congress to abolish slavery in all thirteen states. Three years prior to this proposal, Jefferson had made known his feelings against slavery in his book *Notes on the State of Virginia (1781)*, widely circulated across the nation:

"The whole commerce between master and slave is a perpetual exercise of the most boisterous passions, the most unremitting despotism on the one part, and degrading submissions on the other." [11]

Jefferson's proposed law stated in part that:

"... After the year 1800 of the Christian era, there shall be neither slavery nor involuntary servitude in any of the said States, otherwise than in punishment of crimes, whereof the party shall have been duly convicted to have been personally guilty." [12]

When the votes were cast, U.S. lawmakers came within one vote of completely outlawing slavery in all future states beyond the original thirteen. Why one vote short? The congressman from New Jersey was home sick!

Like Washington, Jefferson had planned on freeing his slaves in his Will. However, the Virginia Legislature passed a new law that essentially prohibited him from doing so. The law stated in part:

"It shall be lawful for any person, by his or her last will and testament, or by any other instrument in writing under his or her hand and seal...to emancipate and set free his or her slaves...Provided, also, that all slaves so emancipated, not being...of sound mind and body, or being above the age of forty-five years, or being males under the age of twenty one, or females under the age of eighteen years, shall respectively be supported and maintained by the person so liberating them, or by his or her estate." [13]

Clearly this was legislation designed to prevent the liberating of slaves. Who would agree to such restrictions?

In 1808 Congress officially banned the *importation* of slaves, though slavery did continue in those states where the institution was legal. The Clotilde was the last ship to bring slaves to U.S. soil. It arrived in Mobile Bay, Alabama, where her captain abandoned her and the slaves escaped, many settling at a place later called Africatown.

CHAPTER 3

THE PRE-CHAD ELECTION ELECTION

AND THE BAND PLAYED ON

America, a rollicking, bustling growing young giant, like a youngster in a growth spurt outgrowing his coveralls, was striving to reach full growth; immigrants were flocking to its shores; industry was near world-class standards in the North; cotton and tobacco fueled the growth of southern plantations. The West was opening up and pioneers were on the move. America, heart of the English speaking New World, was a land fraught with opportunity ~ for good and evil.

THE PRE-CHAD ELECTION ELECTION

As George Washington is recognized as the Father of our country, Thomas Jefferson could be credited with being the father of our modern political system. The Democratic-Republican Party, founded by Jefferson in 1793, ultimately became the source of both parties. John Quincy Adams, Andrew Jackson, John C. Calhoun, Martin Van Buren, and Henry Clay all campaigned as Democratic-Republicans and John Quincy Adams was elected President on the Democratic-Republican ticket. The controversy surrounding his election became the impetus for the modern Democrat Party.

The election of 1824, with candidates John Quincy Adams (MA), Andrew Jackson (TN), William Crawford (GA), and Henry Clay (KY) produced a major electoral college/popular vote controversy. Jackson won the popular vote and 99 electoral votes; Adams had 84 electoral votes; Crawford, 41; and Clay, 37. Since no candidate had the requisite 131 electoral votes, the winner would be determined by the House of Representatives as specified by the Twelfth Amendment. The electoral votes would be disregarded. There were 24 states, each with one vote. After a furious debate, the House decided ~ Jackson collected seven votes; Crawford, four; and Adams 13. On February 9, 1824, Adams became President. Jackson, determined to capture what he viewed as "stolen" (where have we heard that before?), set about building a political coalition to take the White House in 1828. The modern Democrat Party was actually formed from a base of unhappy Democratic-Republicans. The "house that Jackson built" later dropped "Republican" and adopted the name "Democrat."

GO WEST, YOUNG MAN

GOLD!!! The Gold Rush of 1849 blew open the doors to the West. Politicians constantly campaigned for the settlement of these vast new uncharted territories rich with the promise of large plantations, even though by then the importation of slaves was legally banned. Most of the Founders had died, and while there remained an intense aversion toward slavery in the North, that was not the case in the southern states.

Politics is the art of compromise. After fierce congressional debate over the expansion of slavery into the new federal territories, Congress passed the Missouri Compromise - for every slave state allowed into the Union, a free state would enter. Missouri, for instance, would be admitted as a slave state, and Maine as a free state, thus maintaining the one-to-one balance of "slave" versus "free" states. Though the Missouri Compromise also banned slavery in the recent Louisiana Purchase that was not the end of the story. The increase of slave state representation in Congress, coupled with a desire to facilitate growth in the western territories, resulted in the passage of the Kansas-Nebraska Act. This legislation repealed the Missouri Compromise and its ban on slavery in the Louisiana Purchase and would now allow each new territory to determine its own slave or free state status. "Honest Abe" Lincoln did not think that wise, and had this to say in a speech concerning the Kansas Nebraska Act:

"...But it is said, there now is no law in Nebraska on the subject of slavery...That is good book-law; but is not the rule of actual practice. Wherever slavery is, it has been first introduced without law. The oldest laws we find concerning it, are not laws introducing it; but regulating it, as an already existing thing...The difficulty in removing it will carry the vote in its favor. Keep it out until a vote is taken, and a vote in favor of it cannot be got in any population of forty thousand on earth...who have been drawn together by the ordinary

motives of emigration and settlement. To get slaves…into the country…in the incipient stages of settlement is the precise stake played for and won in this Nebraska measure." [1]

An old Middle Eastern proverb says, *"Do not permit the camel to get his nose in your tent"* ~ once the nose, then the hump, with the hump comes the rump, and soon you will have a camel in your tent." It works that way in politics, too. Lincoln knew, as did many others, that Kansas-Nebraska was the "camel's nose."

The country was already deeply divided on the issue of slavery when two new and major issues surfaced, one judicial and one legislative. The *Dred Scott Decision* and *The Fugitive Slave Act* both actively involved the average white American and would further erode the rights of black Americans. Both were as vigorously supported by the Democrats as opposed by the Republicans.

CHAPTER 4

BY ORDER OF THE SUPREME COURT... "NEGROES INFERIOR"

DRED SCOTT... CITIZEN?

[Negroes]*"... so far inferior, that they had no rights which the white man was bound to respect; and that the Negro might justly and lawfully be reduced to slavery for his benefit."* [1]

(U.S. Supreme Chief Justice Taney, 1857)

For Blacks, besides the Johnson vs. Casor decision giving judicial approval to slavery, the Dred Scott vs. Sanford case was one of the most pivotal cases ever tried in the United States.

Dred Scott was property. He was born in Virginia as a slave of the Peter Blow family. In 1830, the Blows moved to St. Louis and took Dred Scott with them. Financial problems forced the Blows to sell Scott to Dr. John Emerson, a military surgeon, who took Scott with him to several outposts. This is significant because one of the outposts was in the Wisconsin territory and the Missouri Compromise prohibited slavery there. Dr. Emerson married Irene Sanford and they took the Scotts back to St. Louis where Emerson died the following year. On April 6th, 1846, Dred Scott, who had married Harriet Robinson, a slave, and had two children, filed suit against Irene Emerson for their freedom. Scott was 50 years old and had lived as a slave in free territories for about nine years. It is possible that free Blacks or abolitionists may have encouraged the suit on the grounds that Missouri courts would support the doctrine of "once free, always free." It is doubtful the Scotts could have afforded to pursue the lawsuit from their own resources. The children of Scott's original owners backed them financially and supported them through years of complicated legal strategies.

It is difficult for us to comprehend today, but in 1846 the issue was not the Scotts' freedom but the *property rights* of the owners. Slaves were property, like a car or expensive motor home today. Let's say you drove your motor home from Missouri to Wisconsin and that state claimed it was illegal to own a motor home there. Should the courts appropriate the vehicle when you get back to Missouri? In 1877, very few white inhabitants of slave states considered the human factor in this case. Dred Scott *belonged* to Mrs. Emerson. Today, it is universally acknowledged that slavery was wrong, but these were the pertinent issues in the Dred Scott case. It was all about property rights.

The Scotts went to court and lost, but a judge later granted a second trial. In the second trial, the jury decided in favor of Scott and his family, but Emerson appealed; she did not want to lose her property. In 1852, the Missouri State Supreme Court ruled in Emerson's favor, reversing the lower court's ruling. The case went to federal court when Scott's new team of lawyers, passionately opposed to slavery, appealed to the U.S. Supreme Court. On March 6th, 1857, Chief Justice Roger B. Taney, a staunch and public advocate of slavery, delivered the personally written majority opinion of the U.S. Supreme Court:

> *"The question is simply this: Can a negro, whose ancestors were imported into this country, and sold as slaves, become a member of the political community formed and brought into existence by the Constitution of the United States, and as such become entitled to all the rights, and privileges, and immunities, guarantied by [the Constitution] to the citizen? One of which rights is the privilege of suing in a court of the United States in the cases specified in the Constitution. We think they [negroes] are not, and that they are not included, and were not intended to be included, under the word "citizens" in the Constitution, and can therefore claim none of the rights and privileges which it [the Constitution] provides for...citizens of the United States...the public history of every European nation displays it in a manner too plain to be mistaken. They [Negroes] had for more than a century been regarded as beings of an inferior order, and altogether unfit to associate with the white race, wither in social or political relations; and so far inferior, that they had no rights which the white man was bound to respect; and that the negro might justly and lawfully be reduced to slavery for his benefit."* [2]

Seven of the nine justices agreed ~ *Scott had never been free; slaves were personal property; the Missouri Compromise was unconstitutional; and the federal government had no right to prohibit slavery in the new territories.* The Scotts were subsequently returned to Irene

Emerson...and slavery. There are two ironic footnotes to these proceedings. Irene Emerson married Calvin C. Chaffee, a northern Congressman who was strongly opposed to slavery. Shortly after her marriage, Mrs. Emerson-Chaffee released the Scott family to the Blows, who freed him immediately. Dred Scott became a free man. Nine months later, Dred Scott died.

FUGITIVES OR LEGISLATIVE SLAVES?

With the Compromise of 1850, a major threat to the Union - secession by slave-owning states - was resolved (at least postponed) and the nation remained intact. However, one of the bills in the compromise package, The Fugitive Slave Act, had an unforeseen consequence for the slave states; it further galvanized resistance to slavery. People who were neutral were now required to participate in the perpetuation of slavery by helping to capture runaways. The Underground Railroad flourished. Thousands took strong definitive positions for or against the institution, and the abolitionists' forces gained members, money, and momentum. In the following decade, the nation would become bitterly divided over the issue of slavery, and the rift would expand until the nation divided itself.

A series of bills designed to address several serious regional and territorial issues made up the Compromise of 1850. The Fugitive Slave Act caused an immediate uproar. The provisions of this one particular act were most controversial because:

- It required all citizens to assist in the recovery of fugitive slaves

- It denied a fugitive's right to a jury trial

- It appointed special commissioners to handle the cases

These commissioners would be paid $5 if an alleged fugitive was released and $10 if sent away with the person making the claim. Many free Blacks were illegally captured and sent south into slavery; thousands fled to Canada, but others were not as fortunate. For ex-slaves and many free Blacks attempting to build lives in the North, the new law was disaster.

THEN THERE WERE TWO

In 1854, in Wisconsin, a group of likeminded citizens calling themselves "Democratic-Republicans" formed a new political party specifically to prevent the spread of slavery into the new federal territories. In July of that same year, at their state convention in Jackson, Michigan, they formally adopted their new name ~ Republicans. This new Republican Party founded squarely on opposition to slavery, found the oratory of a lanky backwoods country lawyer extremely compelling. Though defeated in a race for the Senate, Abraham Lincoln's "plainspeak" made him a favorite among these new Republicans. It has been popularly reported that the Republican Party is the "party of Lincoln," but Lincoln is also the creation of the Republican Party. Of the seventeen planks in their platform, seven, directly or indirectly, called for the abolition of slavery. Should Republicans carry the day, there was little doubt as to their intent.

WAR...HUH...WHAT IS IT GOOD FOR?
~ '60s anti-war anthem

In the 1860 presidential elections, there were three major issues on people's minds:

1. The Fugitive Slave Act

2. The Dred Scott Decision

3. Secession

In this one instance there would be no question, no doubt; with Lincoln heading the ticket, Republicans would be clear and outspoken in their opposition to slavery. The people, not polls, would speak. At their national convention, the Republicans nominated Abraham Lincoln for president, and after only six years in existence, captured the presidency and the majority in Congress. Although Lincoln won only 39% of the popular vote, he carried all eighteen free states with their 180 electoral votes. With the election of Lincoln, an outspoken opponent of slavery, secession by the slave states was a foregone conclusion. South Carolina was joined by other southern states in adopting a provisional constitution for a new entitiy called "The Confederate States of America." Jefferson Davis was elected and would serve as their President.

On March 4, 1861, Lincoln closed his inaugural address with *"a plea for restoration of the bonds of union," and* declared seccession *"legally void."* Nearly every Democrat bolted Congress to serve in the "new government." On April 12th the first shots of the Civil War were fired at Ft. Sumter, SC. America was at war with herself.

LINCOLN WASN'T REALLY FOR FREEING SLAVES

Today, Lincoln is sometimes charged with gross hypocrisy. Black critics claim he was not really for freeing *all* slaves; he was only freeing "those he had no power to free." Lincoln never wavered about what he considered to be his primary duty. According to him, the "paramount object" was his constitutional responsibility to the Union. Acutely aware of the South's dependency on slavery, Lincoln, who sought an early end to the war, consulted his Cabinet about an "Emancipation Proclamation." He would challenge the Confederacy: If they do not *"...surrender by January 1, 1863, the President will free all slaves in Confederate territory."* The Confederates refused, and Lincoln formally issued the Emancipation Proclamation:

> *"Now, therefore, I, Abraham Lincoln, President of the United States, by virtue of the power in me vested as Commander in Chief of the Army and Navy of the United States in time of actual armed rebellion against the authority and Government of the United States, and as fit and necessary war measure for suppressing this rebellion, do on this 1st day of January A.D. 1863...order and designate as the States and parts of States wherein the people thereof respectively are this day in rebellion against the United States...I do order and declare that all persons held as slaves within said designated States and parts of States are and hence forward shall be free..."* [3]

It is easy to sit, as many do, in an intellectual ivory tower, and criticize Lincoln from the vantage point of 200 years. Liberal activists and critics of the president appear to be oblivious to the truth that had the South been victorious, all Blacks would today be slaves. Apparently, even hindsight does not necessarily endow wisdom. Lincoln has been harshly criticized for freeing "only those he had no power to free" - the Confederate slaves. His actions, in light of conditions existing at the time, can be seen as a politically sound strategy. Lincoln was not engaged in some civil rights demonstration, but a bloody civil war to determine whether or not the Union, The United States of America, would survive.

There were specific reasons why Lincoln's proclamation did not include the Border States. His clear and legitimate objective was to prevent the slave-owning Border States from joining the Confederacy. Lincoln, I believe, knew that as word filtered down, slaves would draw no clear-cut distinction between southern or Border States. Slaves, wherever they were, upon hearing of emancipation, would scarcely ask their masters for a boundary ruling. They would simply assume their freedom and slip away. There is also additional criticism that Lincoln was inconsistent in some of his policies and positions on slavery. Lincoln was always unequivocal about what he perceived to be his primary role - to save the Union. Had he been able to save the Union without firing a single shot, he would have. Instead, he sent tens of thousands of young men to their deaths.

Lincoln's reply to a friend, a newspaper editor who had editorialized about these policies, clarifies his position:

Executive Mansion,
Washington, August 22, 186

Hon. Horace Greeley:

Dear Sir.

I have just read yours of the 19th. Addressed to myself through the New-York Tribune. If there be in it any statements, or assumptions of fact, which I may know to be erroneous, I do not, now and here, controvert them. If there be in it any inferences which I may believe to be falsely drawn, I do not now and here, argue against them. If there be perceptible [sic] in it an impatient and dictatorial tone, I waive it in deference to an old friend, whose heart I have always supposed to be right. As to the policy I "seem *to be pursuing"* as you say, I have not meant to leave any one in doubt. I would save the Union. I would save it the shortest way under the Constitution. The sooner the national authority can be restored; the nearer the Union will be "the Union as it was." If there be those who would not save the Union, unless they could at the same time save slavery, I do not agree with them. If there be those who would not save the Union unless they could at the same time destroy slavery, I do not agree with them. My paramount object in this struggle is to save the Union, and is not either to save or to destroy slavery. If I could save the Union without freeing any slave I would do it, and if I could save it by freeing all the slaves I would do it; and if I could save it by freeing some and leaving others alone I would also do that. What I do about slavery, and the colored race, I do because I believe it helps to save the Union; and what I forbear, I forbear because I do not believe it would help to save the Union. I shall do less whenever I shall believe what I am doing hurts the cause, and I shall do more whenever I shall believe doing more will help the cause. I shall try to correct errors when shown to be errors; and I shall adopt new views so fast as they shall appear to be true views.*

I have here stated my purpose according to my view of official duty; and I intend no modification of my oft-expressed personal wish that all men everywhere could be free. [4] (emphasis added)

Yours,

A. Lincoln

CHAPTER 5

WHAT DO YOU PEOPLE WANT?

FORTY ACRES AND A MULE

The war was long, bitter, and costly ~ in dollars and lives. Many were asking, "Were these slaves really worth all this?"

Confederate Dead - Antietam, MD - September 1862 [1]

Over four million Americans, North and South, black and white, fought over 10,000 battles. It is difficult, if not impossible, for the modern reader to grasp the emotional trauma generated by the war. The numbers of those killed or wounded are simply staggering. At the pivotal battle of Gettysburg, over 157,000 men fought for three days with more than 50,000 casualties.[2] Some experts place the toll of Civil War dead at almost 700,000. If the same percentage of today's population were killed, it would be the equivalent of five million deaths. According to the best estimates, the battlefield deaths in the Civil War equaled a number greater than all the actual battle deaths suffered by the United States from the Revolution through Vietnam.[3]

The Civil War was a terrible, heart wrenching experience.

I am sure the cries of "bring our boys home" rang with significantly more sincerity and fervor than is contained in many of the anti-war demonstrations covered on national TV today... always carefully edited so their small size and rabid anti-Americanism is not readily evident. As is often the case in a conflict involving American lives, when a solution is not immediately evident, a sitting president may find his popularity has waned somewhat. The elections of 1864 were drawing near and then, as now, *special interest groups* pursued their agendas. (This is a label carefully applied to groups supporting the *opposition*, as one's *own* support groups are never called "special interests.") Character assassination and labeling are not the invention of today's media pundits; today's political critics have merely lowered it to a new level.

To strengthen his appeal in the Border States, Lincoln chose Senator Andrew Johnson of Tennessee as his running mate. Johnson, a moderate Democrat, strongly opposed secession and criticized his fellow Democrats for attempting to destroy the Union.

With a pro-slave southerner (to reassure slave owners in the Border States) as his running mate, Lincoln easily won re-election.

Confederate resistance was waning, and General William Tecumseh Sherman marched almost unopposed through Georgia on his famous, or infamous, (depending on your position vis-à-vis the Mason-Dixon Line) march to the sea. Sherman's army encountered, and was followed by, thousands of slaves freed both by Lincoln's Proclamation and the advancing Union armies. Sherman's dilemma was — what do we do with these thousands of freedmen? Would the slaves be able in any way to help themselves? The root of the dilemma was the misconception held by many (even today) that all slaves were illiterate, helpless, childlike, and completely dependent on "Massa." People who hold this view are either unaware, or have forgotten, that there were many highly skilled slaves who worked as merchants, tradesmen, craftsmen, and even tutors.

November 1868 - These slaves from East Africa are pictured on the lower deck of the Royal Naval ship HMS Daphne. They were taken on board from an Arab slave ship.

Branded, chained together, and shipped in a variety of ways, the cargo - future slaves - survived disease, suffocation, slavers' brutality, and their subsequent slave status. While approximately 20 million Blacks were stolen, captured, or sold into slavery, only about 600,000-800,000 actually arrived in the American Colonies.

Millions died before reaching the Americas and the worst part of the journey had not even begun. The survivors were prime examples of the "survival of the fittest." Only the strongest survived. They were not apt to be as they have often been depicted. The media inaccurately portrays the slave, inadvertently or otherwise, as docile darkies, carefree, child-like and happy, singing in three-part harmony on the way to the cotton fields. There were, perhaps, some of these, but as a general rule, this was most definitely not the case. The happy-go-lucky, singin', tap-dancin' darkie is purely a creation of a fevered imagination depicting a *fictionalized gracious southern* way of life ~ "Lawsy-me, Miz Scarlett!"

The overwhelming majority of Blacks hated slavery and despised Massa. Slaves forced to work in the kitchens would prepare food with deliberately soiled hands after relieving themselves (slaves were given no toilet paper), they dredged up and spat great gobs of phlegm into their master's food, and rubbed food on their unwashed private parts prior to serving it. There were constant open or covert acts of rebellion. They killed themselves, ran away, and died in the swamps or forests. On occasion, they openly revolted and killed their masters. In Virginia alone, 346 slaves were convicted of murder. There are over 90 convictions for insurrection recorded. It is estimated that there were three to four million slaves spread across the South; the possibility of uprisings was a constant concern. It was *not* a happy time.

Most slaves continuously sought a means of escape. When word of "manseepaashun" spread through the South, many of the tough, work-hardened, independent slaves simply walked off the plantations and farms with only the clothes on their backs. Sherman contacted Washington regarding this situation and "Father Lincoln" (African term of respect) acted quickly. He dispatched his Secretary of War, "Radical" Republican Edwin M.

Stanton, who immediately set up a meeting between General Sherman, several black pastors, and himself. The following is a partial transcript of that meeting and is well worth the reading, as it gives insight into the mindset of the slave and their position regarding federal assistance:

HEADQUARTERS OF MAJ. GEN. SHERMAN, CITY OF SAVANNAH, GEORGIA

Jan. 12, 1865 - 8 P.M.

On the evening of Thursday, the twelfth day of January, 1865, the following persons of African descent met by appointment to hold an interview with Edwin M. Stanton, Secretary of War, and Major-Gen. Sherman, to have a conference upon matters relating to the freedmen of the State of Georgia. Twenty church officers and ministers, comprised of fifteen ex-slaves, and five freeborn Blacks were in attendance. Garrison Frazier, an ordained Baptist minister, "being chosen by the persons present to express their common sentiments upon the matters of inquiry, makes answers... as follows:"

MINUTES OF AN INTERVIEW BETWEEN THE COLORED MINISTERS AND CHURCH OFFICERS AT SAVANNAH WITH THE SECRETARY OF WAR AND MAJOR GENERAL SHERMAN
(Excerpted)

<u>Question:</u> STATE WHAT YOUR UNDERSTANDING IS IN REGARD TO THE ACTS OF CONGRESS AND PRESIDENT LINCOLN'S [EMANCIPATION] PROCLAMATION

ANSWER: *So far as I understand President Lincoln's proclamation to the rebellious states, it is, that if they would lay down their arms and submit to the laws of the United States before the first of January, 1863, all should be well; but if they did not, then all the slaves in the rebel states should be free henceforth and forever. That is what I understood.*

QUESTION: STATE WHAT YOU UNDERSTAND BY SLAVERY AND THE FREEDOM THAT WAS TO BE GIVEN BY THE PRESIDENT'S PROCLAMATION.

ANSWER: *Slavery is receiving by irresistible power the work of another man and not by his consent. The freedom, as I understand it, promised by the proclamation, is taking us from under the yoke of bondage and placing us where we could reap the fruit of our own labor, take care of ourselves, and assist the government in maintaining our freedom.*

QUESTION: STATE IN WHAT MANNER YOU THINK YOU CAN TAKE CARE OF YOURSELVES, AND HOW CAN YOU BEST ASSIST THE GOVERNMENT IN MAINTAINING YOUR FREEDOM.

ANSWER: *The way we can best take care of ourselves is to have land, and turn it and till it by our own labor – that is, by the labor of the women and children and old men; and we can soon maintain ourselves and have something to spare...and to assist the government, the young men should enlist in the service of the government... we want to be placed on land until we are able to buy it and make it our own.*

QUESTION: DO YOU THINK THAT THERE IS INTELLIGENCE AMONG THE SLAVES OF THE SOUTH TO MAINTAIN THEMSELVES UNDER THE

GOVERNMENT OF THE UNITED STATES AND THE EQUAL PROTECTION OF ITS LAWS...?

ANSWER: *I think there is sufficient intelligence among us to do so.*

QUESTION: WHAT IS THE FEELING OF THE BLACK POPULATION OF THE SOUTH TOWARD THE GOVERNMENT OF THE UNITED STATES; WHAT IS THEIR UNDERSTANDING IN RESPECT TO THE PRESENT WAR — ITS CAUSES AND OBJECT...STATE FULLY YOUR VIEWS.

ANSWER: *I think you will find...thousands that are willing to make any sacrifice to assist the government of the United States...also many that are not willing to take up arms. I do not suppose there are a dozen men that are opposed to the government. I understand, as to the war, that the South is the aggressor. President Lincoln was elected President by a majority of the United States. The South, without knowing what he would do, rebelled. The Rebels commenced the war before he came into office. The object of the war was not at first to give the slaves their freedom, but the object of the war was at first to bring the rebellious states back into the union and their loyalty to the laws of the United States. Afterward, knowing the value set on the slaves by the rebels, the President thought that his proclamation would stimulate them to lay down their arms, reduce them to obedience, and help to bring back the rebel states; and their not doing so has now made the freedom of the slaves a part of this war...if the prayers that have gone up for the Union Army could be read out, you would not get through them these two weeks.*[4]

Clearly these Blacks did not view themselves as wards of the state, were not seeking a government handout, and did not desire or expect to be looked after by another master. Partially as a result of that meeting, and partially as a result of President Lincoln's reconstruction plan, Sherman issued the following Special Orders:

IN THE FIELD, SAVANNAH, GA., JANUARY 16TH 1865. SPECIAL FIELD ORDERS, NO. 15

I.   The islands from Charleston, South, the abandoned rice fields along the rivers for 30 miles back from the sea, and the country bordering the St. Johns River, Florida, are reserved and set apart for the settlement of the Negroes now made free by the acts of war and the proclamation of the President of the United States.

II. At Beaufort, Hilton Head, Savannah, Fernandina, St. Augustine and Jacksonville, the Blacks may remain in their chosen or accustomed vocations – but on the islands, and in the settlements hereafter to be established, no white person whatever...will be permitted to reside; and the sole and exclusive management of affairs will be left to the freed people themselves, subject only to the United States military authority and the acts of Congress. By the laws of war, and the orders of the President of the United States, the Negro is free and must be dealt with as such...

III. Whenever three respectable Negroes, heads of families, shall desire to settle on land, and shall have selected...locality clearly defined...the inspector of settlements and plantations will...give them a license to settle...and afford such assistance as he can to enable them to establish a peaceable, agricultural settlement. The three parties named will subdivide land...among themselves...so that each family shall have a plot of not more than (40) Forty Acres of tillable ground...the military authorities shall afford them protection, until such time as they can protect themselves...

IV. Whenever a Negro has enlisted in the military service of the United States, he may locate his family in any one of the settlements at pleasure, and acquire a homestead, and all other rights and privileges of a settler, as though present in person...

V. In order to carry out this system...Inspector of Settlements and Plantations...and will furnish personally to each head of a family...a possessory title in writing, giving as near as possible the description of boundaries; the same general officer will also be charged with...protecting their interests while absent from their settlements...

VI. Brigadier General R. Saxton is hereby appointed Inspector of Settlements and Plantations, and will at once enter on the performance of his duties...[5]

Land was clearly and unmistakably set aside for *ownership* by these freedmen.

Each family was to receive forty acres of land and "such animals as would not be useful to the army, a horse or a mule." With the war drawing to a close, the ex-slaves could use the mules and horses no longer needed by the Army. This is most likely the origin of the phrase "Forty Acres and a Mule." By the summer of 1865, 40,000 freed men had received approximately 400,000 acres of abandoned Confederate land.

MAKING IT LEGAL

When the meeting of General Sherman, Secretary of War Stanton, and the black leaders took place, Congress, unsure of the Lincoln's authority to issue the Emancipation Proclamation, had as yet taken no official steps regarding the freed slaves. To address this issue, they proposed the 13th Amendment abolishing slavery. The majority of the Democrats had gone south, but a few remained in the Congress. As to where their loyalties lie, the following would smoke them out:

THE 13TH AMENDMENT

Neither slavery nor involuntary servitude, except as a punishment for crime whereof the party shall have been duly convicted, shall exist within the United States, or any place subject to their jurisdiction. (Ratified 1865)

As for the argument, "That was all in the past," it is well to remember that *those who forget the past are doomed to repeat it.* The sad fact is that the Democrat Party, every year from 1865 to 1965, not only debated, but fought with guns and every procedural weapon at their disposal to prevent Blacks from enjoying full citizenship.

In December 1865, Democrat opposition notwithstanding, the 13th Amendment was ratified. Only the third amendment since the Bill of Rights, it abolished slavery in the United States and its territories forever. Millions of slaves were suddenly thrust into the economy with only the clothes on their backs. This was only one of the problems facing Congress after the war. Keep in mind, the South, lacking the industrial strength and manufacturing capacities of the North, was devastated by the war. Many Whites were not much better off than some of the slaves, and others, lacking skills possessed by some slaves, were worse off. The currency had no value, crops were destroyed, thousands of men had been killed, and the planter class decimated. To address these problems, Congress established **The Bureau of Refugees, Freedmen, and Abandoned Lands**, a temporary agency commonly called **"The Freedmen's Bureau."**

On the national level, all lands, either confiscated by the Union or abandoned by the Confederates, came under the jurisdiction of the Freedmen's Bureau. General Oliver Otis Howard (who later founded Howard University in Washington, D.C.) headed the Bureau. Set up primarily to provide temporary relief in the form of food, basic shelter, medical care, assistance in labor-contract negotiation, establishment of schools, and similar services to Blacks, the Bureau helped thousands of southern Whites as well. Possessing little more than the ex-slaves, all the southern White had, in many cases, was his "whiteness." Rabble-rousers would soon utilize this similarity of circumstance to generate the racial divide that was to become the basis for the "black codes" and segregation.

REPATRIATION

Lincoln never indicated any desire to penalize the South. His goal now was to restore the Union he fought to preserve and seek ways to heal and repatriate the South.

He proposed, among other things...

- A general amnesty; one-tenth of the voters must take an oath of loyalty to the United States and pledge to obey all federal laws pertaining to slavery

- Temporary exclusion of high Confederate officials and military leaders from government positions

- States would create a new government and elect representatives to Congress.

As a result of the first provision, the plan was dubbed the "Ten Percent Plan." A powerful coalition of Republicans in Congress opposed this plan as, in their view, it failed to safeguard the rights of black citizens and left the architects of secession in power. This group favored not only the abolition of slavery, but complete equality for the ex-slaves. This radical notion earned the group the nickname "Radical Republicans." Long before it was politically correct, and with little or nothing to be gained by supporting the right of slaves to full citizenship, these men were determined to bring Blacks into the mainstream. Although revisionist historians attempt to portray them as right wing extremists and obstructionists determined to punish the South, the charge is utterly without merit. As a general rule, they felt little compulsion to punish, but felt the South should not be rewarded with leniency for attempting to destroy the Union. Joined by some moderate Republicans, the radicals refused to pass Lincoln's Ten Percent Plan and passed their own, the more stringent Wade-Davis Bill. It required, among other things, 50% of a state's white males to take an ironclad oath that they had never supported the rebellion. In addition, for readmission to the Union, states were required to give Blacks the right to vote. President Lincoln chose not to sign it, killing the bill with a pocket veto.

In April 1865, at the old Court House in Appomattox, Virginia, General Robert E. Lee surrendered his armies to General Ulysses S. Grant, ending the most costly war, in terms of human lives, in which America has ever been involved, before or since. The Civil war was ended, the Union was saved, and Lincoln was vindicated.

That same month of that same year President Abraham Lincoln was assassinated.

CHAPTER 6

A LEOPARD WITHOUT SPOTS

RECONSTRUCTION

Vice President Andrew Johnson became the new President. It has been reported that Johnson merely carried out Lincoln's plan for Reconstruction, but this was not the case, as Johnson had his own agenda. He had opposed secession but never wavered from being a devout believer in slavery; and, he blamed the rich white planter class for the Civil War.

Johnson never had any inclination to end slavery and no predisposition to alleviate the burdens of the new freedmen. Born a poor illiterate from the South, he planned to advance poor southern Whites using federal lands and pardons as his vehicle. With Congress in recess, Johnson implemented his own reconstruction policy. No allegiance to the Union was required, and just a simple oath that said, in effect, "we're sorry" qualified for a special pardon. He handed out thousands of these special pardons, and began returning captured federal land to the ex-Confederates. When General Howard, head of the Freedmen's Bureau, learned of Johnson's actions, he immediately issued Circular #13, awarding the freedmen their forty acres. He intended to get the land into their hands as soon as possible.

Meanwhile, in Washington, Johnson continued with his plans. The rich planter classes (those with over $20,000 in assets) whom he blamed for the war, were required to personally write or come to "beg pardon." He issued pardons to all who came including many former Confederate government officials and officers. Johnson allowed these "repatriated citizens" to adopt new state constitutions and establish new state governments. Despite any animosity he may have felt toward them, he was convinced that only the planter class could maintain order and restore the South. Once restored to power, these former slave masters, in order to "establish and maintain order," immediately enacted rigid, harsh *black codes* that, in effect, simply perpetuated slavery under another name.

Following are samples of some of these codes:

Blacks:

- Were required to secure permission to come into town (the permission slip had to give the nature of the visit and the length of the expected stay)

- Could be imprisoned if discovered out on the street after 10:00 PM without this permission slip

- Could be declared vagrant if determined to be unemployed and/or without permanent residence. If found guilty, they could be "indentured" for an unspecified amount of time.

- Could not dispute the word of Whites
- Could not make insulting noises, or speak disrespectfully or out of turn
- Must stand at attention when Whites passed
- Step aside when white women were on the sidewalk
- Remove their hats in the presence of Whites
- "Apprentice" laws allowed orphans or other children to be hired out to Whites. Many of the *employers* turned out to be their former owners.
- States could determine the type of property and skills Blacks could possess.

These codes often contained a catch-22. For example, Blacks could not possess land outside some cities and at the same time could not live in town. The objective of these codes was to ensure that none became self-sufficient. Back in session, an alarmed Congress viewed Johnson's actions as negating the hard-won victory. The black codes, the refusal of the southern states to ratify the 13th Amendment, and ex-Confederates elected to Congress were all clear indications that this was turning back the clock. Johnson rejected every option the Congress presented for assisting the ex-slaves, including sending them west to settle on government lands. He was determined to keep the freedmen in a dependent condition. When he heard of Circular #13, he immediately ordered Howard to issue Circular #15, voiding any and all previous land transfers, disenfranchising the ex-slaves, making it all but impossible for them to escape their slavery-induced poverty.

Many Blacks to this day believe **Republicans** robbed them of their *forty acres and a mule*. The charges against Republicans and the call for "reparations" are partially based on this belief. However, it was Johnson, a **Democrat**, who ordered General Howard, a Republican, to evict the freedmen from cleared, tilled, and productive land, making it appear the Republicans had defaulted on their promise. If reparations were due, then Democrats should be held accountable, not Republicans.

In 1866, the predominantly Republican Congress was divided into three groups:

1. *Radicals* (who favored the immediate eradication of slavery and full citizenship for Blacks)

2. *Conservatives* (who favored a gradual emancipation)

3. *Moderates* (who favored emancipation with reservations)

Led by the radicals, the Republicans were determined to protect the rights of the freedmen so Congress took several steps immediately to stop the President:

1. They refused to recognize or seat the new Representatives.

2. They ordered the military to protect Blacks from the increasing violence against them (2,000 were murdered in Louisiana alone).

3. They also passed the Freedmen's Bureau Act, extending indefinitely the life of the agency. Johnson vetoed it.

The radicals led the charge for civil rights, including passing the first civil rights act. At the risk of being repetitious, the *rad-*

ical Republicans in Congress (derided as "Black Republicans" in the South) had almost nothing to gain in this battle for the civil rights of some ex-slaves. They were, however, determined to ensure that black Americans were guaranteed equal rights under the law. In support of that position, they passed the following legislation:

THE CIVIL RIGHTS ACT OF 1866:

An Act to protect all Persons in the United States in their Civil Rights and furnish the Means of their Vindication.

Be it enacted by the Senate and House of Representatives of the United States of America in Congress assembled, That all persons born in the United States and not subject to any foreign power, excluding Indians not taxed, are hereby declared to be citizens of the United States; and such citizens of every race and color, without regard to any previous condition of slavery or involuntary servitude, except as a punishment for crime whereof the party shall have been duly convicted, shall have the same right, in every State and Territory in the United States, to make and enforce contracts, to sue, be parties, and give evidence, to inherit, purchase, lease, sell, hold, and convey real and personal property, and to full and equal benefit of all laws and proceedings for the security of person and property, as is enjoyed by white citizens, and shall be subject to like punishment, pains, and penalties, and to none other, any law, statute, ordinance, regulation, or custom, to the contrary notwithstanding.

Johnson vetoed it.

The Republican Congress immediately passed the bill again.

Johnson vetoed it.

Congress overrode his veto.

It was not a matter of punishing the South (although I am sure there were some who felt that was a justifiable course of action); but, Congress, because of a bitter and unpopular war costing the lives of thousands, was determined to see Blacks obtain full citizenship. Slavery had been abolished by the 13th Amendment, but the southern states refused to ratify it and then circumvented its provisions by claiming that slaves, though free, were not citizens. The South cited states' rights (guaranteed by the 10th Amendment) and insisted the federal government had no authority to enforce any civil rights laws. To guarantee citizenship to Blacks, and over-ride the states' rights arguments, Congress proposed the 14th Amendment. This amendment would guarantee equal protection under the law to "all persons."

THE 14TH AMENDMENT

All persons born or naturalized in the United States, and subject to the jurisdiction thereof, are citizens of the United States and of the State wherein they reside. No State shall make or enforce any law, which shall abridge the privileges or immunities of citizens of the United States; nor shall any State deprive any person of life liberty, or property without due process of law; nor deny to any person within its jurisdiction the equal protection of the laws. (1868)

Few things so clearly highlight the differences between the two parties on civil rights as the Congressional Record of the vote for the proposed **14th Amendment**.

For Passage of the 14th Ammendment

SENATE

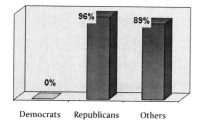

96%   89%   0%

Democrats   Republicans   Others

HOUSE

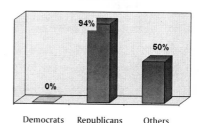

94%   50%   0%

Democrats   Republicans   Others

Much of the country viewed the 1866 congressional elections as a national referendum on the 14th Amendment and northern voters gave the Republicans a clear majority, ensuring they had more than enough votes to override any Presidential veto.

Congress once again passed the Freedmen's Bureau Act.

Johnson vetoed it.

Congress overrode his veto.

In 1867, the Republican-dominated Congress passed legislation that required the southern states to enact new constitutions in line with the 14th Amendment, granting voting rights to black males. Re-admission to the Union required ratification of the 14th Amendment.

Johnson vetoed it.

Congress overrode it.

A LEOPARD WITHOUT SPOTS IS STILL A LEOPARD

The Democrats, now the dominant party in the South, saw the need to alter its strategy. Since only compliance with federal legislation would allow readmission to the Union and representation in Congress, they began to agree to all demands of the Republican Congress. This tactic subsequently increased the number of Democrats in Congress. Tennessee had already returned to the Union; Alabama, Arkansas, Florida, Georgia, Louisiana, North and South Carolina were all re-admitted in June 1868. This may be just an interesting coincidence, but the same month, the same year Democrats returned to Congress, the Freedmen's Bureau ceased to exist.

On July 21, 1868, the 14th Amendment was ratified and became perhaps one of the most significant additions ever to the Constitution of the United States.

CHAPTER 7

MOVING ON

It was time for a new beginning. The slaves were free. Reconstruction, though expensive, and unpopular with some, was well under way. Congress was adamant; slavery would not just continue under a different name, and four Reconstruction acts were passed in support of this position. These acts required, among other things:

- Creation of five military districts

- Registration of voters (including all freedmen and those white men who took the extended loyalty oath)

- New state constitutions providing for black male suffrage

- Ratification of the 14th Amendment

As a direct result of these legislative initiatives, many Blacks were elected to local and national office, including Pinckney Benton Stuart Pinchback, who became the first black governor of any state; he was elected governor of Louisiana in 1872. At the national level, black officeholders, Republicans all, included:

- Joseph H. Rainey (SC) - First black member of the U.S. House of Representatives

- Blanche Kelso Bruce (MS) - Senate, and the first Black to preside over a Senate session; (Bruce received eleven votes for Vice President at the Republican Convention in 1888)

- Hiram Revels (MS) - Senate

- Robert Brown Elliott (SC) - House

An interesting sidebar: Three African-Americans have *presided* over *Republican* National Conventions:

1. Congressman John Roy Lynch -1884 - RNC Chicago

2. Senator Edward Brooke - 1968 - RNC Miami

3. Congressman J.C. Watts, Jr. - 2000 RNC Philadelphia

If the argument were made, "Republicans were only trying to impress Blacks," what would be the Democrats' strategy? Only one African-American, Yvonne Brathwaite-Burke, made it as high as Vice-Chair - not *Co*-Chair but **Vice**-Chair - of a Democratic National Convention. In the "party for the African-Americans," not a single African-American has come close to presiding over a Democratic National Convention.

CROSSING OVER JORDAN

Perhaps I may be forgiven for going on just a bit about some of the men elected to Congress, a few directly from slavery:

THE FIRST COLORED SENATOR AND REPRESENTATIVES ~ 41ST & 42ND CONGRESS OF THE UNITED STATES

Pictured here are Senator Hiram R. Revels and Representatives Benjamin S. Turner, Josiah T. Walls, Joseph H. Rainey, Robert Brown Elliot, Robert D. De Large, and Jefferson H. Long. [1]

One member of Congress deserves an honorable mention. Shortly after former Speaker of the House in South Carolina, Robert Brown Elliott, was elected to the U.S. House of Representatives, he engaged in a debate over a civil rights bill. His opponents, Alexander Hamilton Stephens of Georgia (the Vice-President of the Confederacy, sent to Congress as a Democrat after the Civil War), James Beck (D-KY) and John Thomas Harris (D-VA), attacked the civil rights bill. Here is a portion of Elliot's response:

"Mr. Speaker… it is a matter of regret to me that it is necessary at this day that I should rise in the presence of an

American Congress to advocate a bill which simply asserts rights and equal privileges for all classes of American citizens. I regret, sir, that the dark hue of my skin may lend a color to the imputation that I am controlled by motives personal to myself in my advocacy of this great measure of natural justice. Sir, the motive that impels me is restricted by no such narrow boundary but is as broad as the Constitution...[2]

According to the African Methodist Episcopal Church Review:

"...Democrats...could not deny the merits of his speeches, so they denied his authorship of them...made the charge of non-authorship upon the general principle that the Negro, of himself, could accomplish nothing of literary excellence." [3]

He must have a ghostwriter. There was just no way a Black could be so articulate. (It seems little has changed for liberals and Democrats. According to them, Blacks still can't achieve or be articulate or literate on their own; hence, the change in the original intent of affirmative action.)

Elliott also traveled, spoke to, and worked among the ex-slaves:

"From county to county he traveled, teaching them the first lessons in self-government. They...learned from his lips the principles and deeds of the Republican party which had liberated them and their children from cruel bondage and which was now to give them that silent but potent motive power: the ballot - the safeguard and bulwark of American freedom." [4]

BUSINESS AS USUAL

1869 ~ General Ulysses S. Grant was elected as the 18th President of the United States.

If there is any error to be charged to the Republicans and the North, we come now upon it. The North, eager to get back to normal and come off the emotional roller coaster of war, became concerned with itself. Emotionally exhausted by war, disgusted by scandals in the Grant administration, weary of Reconstruction, and concerned with restoring prosperity, Republicans, then as now, became less than zealous of the vote and returned to business as usual.

Today it appears many Americans may be deceived regarding human nature, but one particularly perceptive congressman clearly was not. Thaddeus Stevens, a radical Republican and dedicated opponent of slavery, had grave concerns regarding the Democrats and the future of black Americans. So fixed was this distrust that he actually favored amending the Constitution to defend against them. One of his major concerns was that Democrats would one day become the majority in Congress and roll back the hard-won civil rights gains of Blacks. In 1865, Stevens said this:

> "...*They* [Confederates] *ought never to be recognized as capable of acting in the Union, or of being counted as valid States, until the Constitution shall have been so amended as to make it what its framers intended...and so as to render our republican Government firm and stable forever. The first of those amendments is to change the basis of representation among the States from Federal numbers to actual voters. With the basis unchanged the 83 Southern members, with the Democrats that*

will in the best times be elected from the North, will always give
a majority in Congress and in the Electoral College... I need not
depict the ruin that would follow..."

Stevens recommended amending the Constitution to eliminate the advantage the Three-Fifth's Clause gave the South.
Stevens was advocating one man/one vote as the actual numbers counted toward electoral votes. The three-fifths provision
gave the South approximately 24 extra seats, which, when
added to the number they would normally receive from free
white voting citizens, would always give them a majority in Congress. Stevens further recommended:

"... This is not all that we ought to do before inveterate rebels
are invited to participate in our legislation. We have turned,
or are about to turn, loose four million slaves without a hut
to shelter them or a cent in their pockets. The infernal laws of
slavery have prevented them from acquiring an education,
understanding the common laws of contract, or of managing
the ordinary business of life.

This Congress is bound to provide for them until they can take
care of themselves. If we do not furnish them with home-
steads, and hedge them around with protective laws; if we
leave them to the legislation of their late masters, we had bet-
ter have left them in bondage. If we fail in this great duty
now, when we have the power, we shall deserve and receive the
execration of history and of all future ages." [5]

In the 1874 mid-term Congressional elections, the Democrat
Party won control of both houses of Congress for the first time
since the Civil War. Less than ten years later, almost as if they

had been Biblical prophecies, the predictions of Thaddeus Stevens materialized and brought with them almost 100 years of suffering for Blacks who would be born in America. Although the Civil War was over, let the record show that in the South there had been no mass conversions. *Southern gentlemen* still favored slavery, and new constitutions could now be ratified by a simple majority vote in each state.

FROM THE GREEK WORD "KUKLOS" (circle) AND KLAN (alternate spelling)
"KU KLUX KLAN" SUGGESTS A CIRCLE OR BROTHERHOOD

It is commonly accepted that six Confederate veterans in Tennessee initially organized the Ku Klux Klan in the mid 1860s as a social fraternity club. However, with secret meetings, coned hats, robes, and disguises they soon attracted the attention and participation of men with more secret than social motives. Former Confederate General Nathan Bedford Forrest (whose troops committed the infamous Fort Pillow Massacre of more than 300 black men, women, and children who had surrendered the fort) likely became The Grand Wizard. The Klan spread like a deadly virus throughout the South to eventually become a literal terrorist organization. They killed Blacks for any reason; talking back to Whites, being too familiar, reading a book, or just for being black. The goal of the KKK was to keep the ex-slaves "in their place." The Klan intimidated tens of thousands of black voters, systematically murdered black politicians and political leaders, lynched teachers and ministers, burned churches, drove black landowners off their land, and murdered those who refused to leave.

One little reported historical fact is that almost 30% of their victims were white. White? Yes, White Republicans; "Nigger lovers" trying to help Blacks obtain the rights guaranteed by the Constitution. According to Tuskegee Institute figures, between the years 1882 and 1951, 4,730 people were lynched in the United States: 3,437 Negro and 1,293 white. The largest number of lynchings occurred in 1892; of the 230 persons lynched that year, 161 were Negroes and 69 were Whites.[6]

The Klan expanded to every southern state and became a Democrat constituency group, helping to elect national and state representatives, sheriffs, judges, and mayors who, along with common criminals, became members of the Klan. Every level of government throughout most of the South, and even the U.S. Congress, owed some allegiance to the Klan. Some southern politicians refused to cooperate or knuckle under, among them leaders in Texas, Arkansas and, strangely enough, Tennessee, the birthplace of the Klan. In the 1870s, radical Republican Governor Edmund Davis (TX) established a state police force similar to what would become the Texas Rangers. This special unit (40% of its membership was black) made thousands of arrests and brought the Klan to a screeching halt in Texas. In North and South Carolina, groups of black and white citizens armed themselves, and when necessary, actually fought the Klan. Republicans in Arkansas and Tennessee authorized special anti-Klan police forces to track down and arrest Klansmen. They were then tried and if found guilty, executed.

However, Democrat legislators were fighting, too. They "lynched" every anti-lynching bill introduced in Congress from 1865 into the 20th century, often resorting to their favorite strategy to kill a bill...the filibuster. For example, when the House of Representatives passed an anti-lynching bill as recently as 1922, southern Democrat senators killed it, arguing it was unconstitutional because "it interferes with local and state authority." In other words, Democrats were insisting that local or state authorities had the legal right and power to allow the lynching of Blacks, and the federal government should not interfere.

By the mid-'30s, a new wave of Klan-inspired terror swept through the black community. In 1939, a song by Jazz singer Billie Holiday ~ *"Strange Fruit"* ~ became the unofficial anthem of the anti-lynch movement.

Southern trees bear a strange fruit,

Blood on the leaves and blood at the root,

Black body swinging in the southern breeze,

Strange fruit hanging from the poplar trees.

Responding to pressure for anti-lynch laws by the NAACP, the House introduced an anti-lynch bill in 1937. Democrats filibustered it to death. The House introduced the same bill in 1940. The Democrats killed it with another filibuster. Let there be no doubt; the Democrats in the South meant business. According to the Congressional Record, the Democrats, either by filibuster or committee, *never allowed a single anti-lynch measure* to become law. As I said, they meant business.

CHAPTER 8

A CIVIL RIGHTS TIMELINE

1964 is traditionally viewed as a watershed year for African-American civil liberties.

Consider:

Whereas it is essential to just government we recognize the equality of all men before the law, and hold that it is the duty of government in its dealings with the people to mete out equal and exact justice to all, of whatever nativity, race, color, or persuasion, religious or political; and it being the appropriate object of legislation to enact great fundamental principles into law: Therefore,

Be it enacted, That all persons within the jurisdiction of the United States shall be entitled to the full and equal enjoyment of the accommodations, advantages, facilities, and privileges of inns, public conveyances on land or water, theaters, and other places of public amusement; subject only to the conditions and limitations established by law, and applicable alike to citizens of every race and color, regardless of any previous condition of servitude.

SEC. 2. That any person who shall violate the foregoing section by denying to any citizen, ... the full enjoyment of any of the accommodations, advantages, facilities, or privileges in said section enumerated, or by aiding or inciting such denial, shall, for every such offense, forfeit and pay the sum of five hundred dollars to the person aggrieved thereby,...and shall also, for every such offense, be deemed guilty of a misdemeanor, and, upon conviction thereof, shall be fined not less than five hundred nor more than one thousand dollars, or shall be imprisoned not less than thirty days nor more than one year...

SEC. 3. That the district and circuit courts of the United States shall have exclusively of the courts of the several States...

SEC. 4. That no citizen possessing all other qualifications which are or may be prescribed by law shall be disqualified for service as grand or petit juror in any court of the United States, or of any State, on account of race, color, or previous condition of servitude; and any officer or other person charged with any duty in the selection or summoning of jurors who shall exclude or fail to summon any citizen for the cause afore-said shall, on conviction thereof, be deemed guilty of a misde-meanor, and be fined not more than five thousand dollars.

SEC. 5. That all cases arising under the provisions of this act...shall be renewable by the Supreme Court of the United States, without regard to the sum in controversy...(emphasis added)

If the language "*... inns, public conveyances on land or water...regardless of any previous condition of servitude...pay the* *sum of five hundred dollars to the person aggrieved thereby"* seems slightly archaic and the fines relatively small, that's because judged by the standards of today they are. This is not the Civil Rights Act of 1964; it is the Civil Rights Act of 1875!! Although the outgoing Republican Congress passed this comprehensive civil rights bill just prior to the Democrats regaining power in 1875, almost a half-century would pass before any significant progress occurred in the arena of civil rights.

A TIMELINE

1619:   First Blacks Arrive

1654:   First Official Slave

1865:   Emancipation Proclamation Issued

1866:   13th Amendment Ratified

1868:   14th Amendment Ratified

1870:   15th Amendment Ratified

1874:   Democrats Regain Congress

1875:   Civil Rights Act Passed By Outgoing Republican Majority

1877:   Democrat "Redeemer Governments" Installed

1878:   Black Codes Instituted

1896:   Plessy V. Ferguson Ruling / Jim Crow Laws

1941:   FDR – Executive Order # 8802 - Defense Contractors (A. Phillip Randolph Threatens March)

1948:   Truman – Executive Order # 9981 - Military Integration (A. Phillip Randolph Threaten Civil Disobedience/No Draft)

1954:   Brown V. Board of Education

1957:   First civil rights act since Reconstruction (Republican sponsored ~ killed by Democrats)

1960:   Civil Rights Act reintroduced by Republican president (killed by Democrats)

1964:   Civil Rights Act

1965:   Voting Rights Act

Historical facts from original sources, along with documented research, show that the Democrat Party has perpetrated virtually every anti-black, pro-segregation legislative initiative from 1871 to 1965. I wondered how they were able to accomplish this.

The 1876 presidential election between candidates Rutherford B. Hayes and Samuel Tilden generated the same type of result as the Bush/Gore 2000 presidential election. As in 2000, Tilden, a Democrat, won the popular vote, but Hayes, a Republican, took the victory with electoral votes. As electoral votes have been, and will be, a continuing subject of debate, let us briefly review the Constitutional provision regarding presidential elections:

U.S. Constitution, Article II, Section 1.(2)

> *Each state shall appoint, in such manner as the Legislature thereof may direct, a number of electors, equal to the whole number of Senators and Representatives to which the State may be entitled in the Congress; but no Senator or Representative, or person holding an office or trust or profit under the United States shall be appointed an elector.*

These electors, known as the Electoral College, are charged with electing the President of the United States. These electors are to be learned individuals elected by an informed citizenry and, therefore, votes cast by these electors would most accurately reflect the wishes of the population of that state.

THE COMPROMISE OF 1877

Politics can be characterized as the art of compromise as there are few things many politicians are unwilling to compromise, including principle. The Hayes-Tilden controversy was based on two issues: (1) The Democrats had won several state elections; (2) the Republicans still controlled the electoral boards. In order to settle the issue, Congress created a fifteen-member electoral commission consisting of ten congressmen and five Supreme Court justices, divided by party, with one independent. When the independent backed out, a Republican replaced him and voted for Hayes, giving Hayes the victory.[1] The Democrats threatened to use their favorite obstructive tactic to prevent Hayes' confirmation - the filibuster (an exceptionally long speech, or a series of speeches which could last for several days).

Compromise was the order of the day. A meeting of the party leaders produced the following compromise; the Democrats would not oppose Hayes if (1) The Republicans would agree to provide investment capital to the South; and (2) The South would be allowed to govern itself; in other words, *home rule.* The Democrats promised to protect the rights of Blacks. (Yeah, right.) The bargain was struck; the commission awarded the election to Hayes who, per the agreement, immediately removed the remaining federal troops from the South, including those Union troops protecting the black legislators in several state houses. *Redeemer Governments* were in ~ civil rights gains were out. These governments stubbornly opposed any possible form of racial equality. White-only redeemer governments, composed mostly of ex-confederate officials, replaced the bi-racial Republican governments voted in during Reconstruction.

Reconstruction had officially ended.

"I'm not a member of any organized political party, I'm a Democrat!"
~ WILL ROGERS

The term "Redeemer" was deliberately chosen because the name was meant to convey the concept that these governments would *redeem,* in the Biblical sense, the South from the *evil grip* of Blacks and Republicans. States not having these Democrat-controlled redeemer governments in power were viewed as being "un-redeemed." These governments saw themselves as saviors, purging the South of the *sin* visited upon it by reconstruction. They viewed northern carpetbaggers [an epithet applied to northern businessmen], southern scalawags [white southerners who supported the Republicans], and black freedmen as the agents of evil. By 1877, these redeemer governments controlled every state in the South.

The "redeemers" viciously repressed the black vote, ran without opposition, and just as Thaddeus Stevens predicted, were re-elected year after year. Since seniority in the U.S. Congress equals power, Democrats soon controlled every committee and systematically refused to enact, enforce, or support any provisions of the 1875 Civil Rights Bill. In 1883, a packed and sympathetic Supreme Court declared the 1875 Civil Rights Act "unconstitutional." Blacks, ever-political pawns, were now subject to the tender mercies of these white-only Democrat governments. Every single black officeholder was removed and all civil rights legislation immediately became null and void. With the redeemer governments firmly in place throughout the South, *not one single piece of civil rights legislation was passed until 1954.* How vastly different America would have been had the Democrats provided even <u>token</u> support for existing legislation.

<u>Consider</u>:

- The 13th Amendment abolished slavery

- The 14th Amendment granted citizenship to Blacks

- The 15th Amendment granted voting rights to black men

- The Civil Rights Act of 1866 guaranteed equal rights and gave the federal courts judicial authority to enforce the act

- The Civil Rights Acts of 1870, 1871, and 1875 granted equality and civil rights

It was not to be. Redeemer governments at the state level, a powerful Democratic bloc at the national level, and a sympathetic Supreme Court ignored, circumvented, or overturned every single civil right guaranteed to Blacks by the amended Constitution.

SEPARATE BUT EQUAL... SEZ WHO?

I was so excited. This was my first train trip. My mother and I were going to visit my Aunt Z.D. and Uncle Cleo in Las Cruces, New Mexico, and we were going on the <u>train</u>! As we boarded the train decades after the fact, we were still walking out the "separate but equal" doctrine in Plessy vs. Ferguson, when, in 1892, Homer Plessy, a Black, was jailed for sitting in the "White" car when he should have been sitting, as we now were, in the "Colored" car. When the train Plessy had boarded reached the Mason-Dixon Line, he was told to move to the "Colored Car." He refused. He was arrested and he later sued. In his initial trial, Judge Ferguson ruled against him and Plessy was found guilty. He appealed to the Supreme Court of Louisiana and lost; he then appealed to the Supreme Court of the United States. Eight of the nine Supreme Court justices ruled against Plessy, basing their decision on the separate-but-equal doctrine...that separate facilities for Blacks and Whites satisfied the 14th Amendment so long as they were equal.[2] The Supreme Court conceded that while the 14th Amendment did establish absolute equality for the races before the law, in what can only be described as tortured logic, they concluded that *"in the nature of things it could not have been intended to abolish distinctions based upon color, or to enforce social, as distinguished from, political equality, or a commingling of the two races unsatisfactory to either."* [3] Therefore, enforced separation was legal and did not stigmatize Blacks because, in the same sense, Whites were forbidden to sit in a railroad car designated for Blacks. All that was required to ensure political equality were *equal facilities*.

The majority decision in Plessy vs. Ferguson served as the basis and legal justification for the racial segregation that, almost a century later, put Mama and me in the "Colored Car" with a greasy bag of fried chicken. The dining car was a "White Car."

CHAPTER 9

HENRY AND THE
HANGING CHAD

Think…about what you tryin' to do to me! ~ Lyrics to R&B
song

It was November 2000, Y2K, and America had just elected a new
Chief Executive, George W. Bush. Beset by controversy, and what
has euphemistically been referred to as "media error," it was one
of the closest elections in modern history. The pronouncements of
Florida Governor Jeb Bush, Florida Secretary of State Kathryn Harris, Rev. Jesse Jackson, various city commissioners, the Florida
Supreme Court, the United States Supreme Court, the voting
machines, and "chads" of every description were all carefully
examined and re-examined. Every possible angle was minutely
scrutinized and debated ad nauseum, save one… possible media
manipulation. Did the media, which by its own admission votes
overwhelmingly Democrat, attempt to influence the election? [1]

I have a question. Can we simply characterize such an amateurish error as calling "Florida for Gore" long before the polls closed "mere media error?" Was anyone fired for such an egregious error? Censored? Chastised? Even asked about it? Can't you just hear the screams of righteous indignation from a *free and unbiased press*? "Media manipulation!" "Outrageous!" "Preposterous!" "Slanderous!"

Unfortunately, Y2K was the first time many Americans learned exactly how their system worked. Most assumed the President was elected directly by popular vote and many were shocked and dismayed to learn electors from each state actually cast the votes for the man who would become president. As is often the case, the hue and cry was not breast beating with chants of "mea culpa, mea culpa" but, as if to prove the wisdom of the Founding Fathers, the "disenfranchised," led by professional agitators, became a mob shouting "off with his head!" Their goal did not seem to be, "let's understand the beauty of our system and work in it," but rather, "let us tear it down and replace it with something else."

When challenged as to what that "something" should be, the rhetoric of the demagogues and their sycophants seemed strangely reminiscent of an old folk song popular in the 60s. It seems a shiftless, lazy Henry, sent for water by his wife Liza, reported the bucket had a hole in it. Her answer was simplicity itself: *Fix it, dear Henry. With what shall I fix it, dear Liza?* Liza continues offering suggestions including cutting straw with *An axe, dear Henry.* Henry then complains of the dullness of the axe, and when Liza suggests he sharpen it, he points out the dry condition of the whetstone. Liza patiently explains he should wet it. *With what shall I wet it, dear Liza? With water, dear Henry. With what shall I fetch it, dear Liza?* Liza, clearly at the end of her patience, snaps, *In the bucket, dear Henry!*…but, in true "it's not our fault, it's the system" style, Henry slyly replies, *There's a h-o-o-o-le in the bucket…*

"It's not our fault…it's the system! We must abolish the Electoral College! People don't understand it, and our democracy is in danger!" It's Kathryn Harris; it's the Bushes; it's the U.S. Supreme Court; it's the Republicans; it's the machines; it's the lack of machines; it's that blankety blank CHAD which had the temerity not to fall out of the hole! *There's a h-o-o-le in the bucket!* All because they didn't take the extra five minutes to learn how to properly execute the single most important right of a citizen in a republic - to vote!

Many American school children graduate from high school with almost no knowledge of the American system of government. According to the Colonial Williamsburg Foundation, only 19% of teenagers could name the three branches of government. (One outstanding example of what American schools once were is "Stonebridge," a school in Chesapeake, Virginia that turns out *scholars*. The children who finish fifth grade there probably know as much about our history as most college students, since American History is no longer required for college graduation.) As this is the case, it should not be surprising that people don't understand the system and, therefore, think our democracy is in danger. Our democracy was never in danger, as America was never intended to be one in the first place. America was founded as, and thus far remains, a republic - for precisely the reasons a democracy fails.

DEMOCRACY: (di-'mä-krə-se)

- Government by the people, exercised either directly or through elected representatives

- The common people, considered as the primary source of political power

- Majority rule

A true democracy is, in effect, mob rule. Any position or person can attain a momentary ascendancy in a democracy. Had America been a true democracy, there could have been a "President Elvis" or the "Beatles" running Congress. Democracies are a good idea in theory, but disastrous in practice.

"Democracies have been found incompatible with personal security or the rights of property; and have in general been as short in their lives as they have been violent in their death."

(James Madison)

REPUBLIC: (ri-'pə-blik)

- Political order in which the supreme power lies in a body of citizens who are entitled to vote for officers and representatives responsible to them

- A nation that has such a political order

In a republic, the individual citizen is responsible for electing representatives to weigh and debate various issues. In a government composed of three branches, the Executive, Legislative, and Judiciary, issues are proposed, weighed, debated, and in some cases enacted into law. The combined efforts and votes of free American citizens elect or re-elect representatives in the person of senators, congressional representatives, and a president. The people give these elected public servants, under the watchful eyes of impartial, constitutionally astute judges, the power to implement the policies necessary to ensure the continued well-being of the world's longest lasting, most stable form of government. However, absent men of integrity in office and high moral standards in the public at large, any form of government, and especially a republic, is destined for chaos. Only someone who has participated fully in the process can know the ineffable privilege, challenges, and rewards of living under our form of government. There are some unique benefits, privileges, and responsibilities associated with the title "American citizen."

Perhaps the single most important freedom yet available to the majority of citizens in America is the right to an unencumbered vote. The right to vote is a hard-won, constitutionally protected right, and should be zealously defended, as it is at the very heart of our republic. Those privileged to vote should do so, only after carefully examining the positions of the political party and politicians campaigning for their vote. Unfortunately, many citizens today who have little, if any, regard for the civic, moral, or religious principles involved simply vote along party lines. If the president were elected solely by the entirety of the population, bloc voting by special interest groups or singular population groups could sway the outcome and disenfranchise the majority of the national population. In 2000, the inordinately high number of people living in cities affected the popular vote, but the greatest number of electoral votes determines the presidency. The people vote to elect representatives who are to carry out their will. Thus, as we have shown, the constitutionally accurate means of electing a president worked to perfection in the Bush/Gore election.

In Hayes/Tilden 1876, as in Bush/Gore 2000, there was a great deal of emphasis on the impact of the outcome on black Americans; subsequently, there was a heavy black voter turnout. In the first election, they voted 99% Republican. That is not a misprint; Blacks at this time were all Republicans. A black Democrat was so rare that the discovery of one actually generated an entry in the Congressional Record. In 1868, Robert Flournoy, during an investigation into the violent activities of the Ku Klux Klan, said:

> *"I am a considerable sort of a Negro man and talk with the Negroes wherever I go. I have never met in all my intercourse with the Negroes of Mississippi but one single Negro who professed to be a Democrat, and that was in the town of Oxford. He was a waiter in a hotel, and he informed me that he was a Democrat. I tried to convert him and failed, and left him a Democrat."* [2]

That black Democrat in the first case was almost as rare as the black Republican, J. C. Watt, in the second. So predictable is the black vote that they are no longer considered simply voters but Democrat voters. As a result, Democrat candidates make cosmetic appearances at black churches and visit Harlem as though anointed by the ghost of Adam Clayton Powell Jr. Democrats apparently require only a token effort to win with their black constituency. It's as though black voters are mesmerized. In 2000, Blacks voted 90% Democrat. It seems difficult to imagine any group today voting in such lockstep. Even the core groups of the Democrat Party — the NEA, the mainstream media, Hollywood elites, certain labor unions, radical environmentalists, and militant homosexuals — do not vote with such uniformity. If 99% of Blacks voted Republican in 1876, and 90% voted Democrat in 2000, the question can be reasonably posed, "What could cause such a seismic shift in the voting patterns of the same ethnic group?"

It is thought that Blacks have always been unaware of the political struggles associated with their fate, but this is not the case. It has consistently been the practice of many, if not most, employers of domestics to act as if these employees were deaf, dumb, and blind. The most intimate details of family and political life were, and are, openly discussed in the presence of domestics. One of my aunts worked in the household of a former Vice President of the United States, and while there were (to my knowledge) no state secrets revealed, many details of other matters were. If I headed an intelligence agency for a foreign government, I would make every effort to subvert the underpaid, underappreciated, unnoticed domestic workers of the world. There are several recorded instances of Blacks, such as Harriet Tubman (the "Black Moses"), serving quite successfully as spies for the Union. A few fawning, foot-shuffling "Yassuhs" to the Confederates and off they went. Slaves, invisible to their owners, learned of, and passed on, all manner of information to the Union forces.

From Lincoln to FDR, Blacks voted exclusively Republican for several very important reasons. To begin with, they knew it was the party of Lincoln, "The Great Emancipator." They were acutely aware that the Republican Party was responsible for their suffrage, and they knew Democrats seceded from the Union rather than face the prospect of freeing their slaves. In addition, southerners hated Yankees and, in most cases, slaves eagerly embraced what "Massa" hated. After the Civil War, the Union Army and the hated-by-"Massa" Scalawags and Carpetbaggers arrived, bringing freedom and, later, citizenship, civil rights, and the power of the vote to Blacks. It required no degree in nuclear physics to determine who to vote for when only one group would allow you to vote. Of course, Blacks voted Republican; Democrats would not allow them to vote.

1 – 2 – 3 SHIFT!

So, exactly what was behind the dramatic shift in the voting patterns of Black America?

Prior to WWII, the U.S. industrial complex was in a buildup and Blacks, moving from the South, encountered the same discrimination in the defense industry they had fled north to escape. Black leaders, led by A. Phillip Randolph and Bayard Rustin, met with the Democrat leadership seeking federal intervention as a solution to the problem. President Franklin Delano Roosevelt and the Democrats refused. Randolph's pleas fell on deaf ears.

But these were new times. A new generation had emerged. Randolph had previously organized and initiated a strike against The Pullman Railroad Car Company, resulting in the founding and establishment of the Brotherhood of Sleeping Car Porters. He knew how to organize and coordinate resistance, and he now had a large affinity group as a base to call upon. Unless FDR's administration took steps to desegregate the industries doing business with the U.S. as defense contractors, Blacks would march on Washington D.C. The march was scheduled for July 1, 1941. By June, there were estimates ranging from 100,000 to upwards of 250,000 potential marchers prepared to descend on the Capitol. Eleanor Roosevelt urged FDR to meet with Randolph and Rustin in an attempt to persuade them to call off the march. Randolph refused. Roosevelt was on the horns of a dilemma. How would the world judge America for condemning Germany's discrimination against the Jews on the one hand, with the Capitol under siege by its own citizens on the other?

Roosevelt, perhaps not a great statesman but ever the astute politician, *saw the light* and issued Executive Order 8802, barring discrimination in the defense industries and all federal bureaus. This executive order also established the Fair Employment Act, which required all federal agencies to negotiate with private employers holding government contracts; a provision that those employers would not "discriminate against persons of any race, color, creed, or nationality in matters of employment." The EO also set up the Fair Employment Practice Committee (FEPC), which would investigate complaints, take steps to eliminate any discrimination, and make recommendations to Roosevelt, himself. This sounded good to Randolph and Rustin, who then called off the march. The younger militants were outraged; "Let us march anyway," they demanded. Randolph, however, insisted the purpose had not been simply to march, but to protest job discrimination, and he felt that FDR had addressed the issue. However, unbeknownst to Randolph and Rustin, while Executive Order 8802 did apply to all defense contractors, in reality it contained no teeth, no enforcement authority.

With the great Black migration shifting the population balances in northern cities, FDR, aware that Blacks tended to vote in greater numbers than Whites in the South, took steps to woo these black voters into the Democrat Party, without alienating his white southern base. He created a black cabinet of advisors (not to be confused with the presidential cabinet); appointed Robert C. Weaver as an aide to the Interior Secretary; placed Mary McLeod Bethune in charge of a "National Youth Administration's Office of Minority Affairs;" and established the interagency

"Department of Negro Affairs." This is the genesis of the practice of what essentially amounts to "buying" the Black vote, and the origin of the myth that the Democrat Party is the refuge of the African-American.

During Roosevelt's re-election campaign, the major black newspapers of the day somehow failed to point out that FDR actually made no new promises to Blacks. While they played up his reputation of eliminating discrimination in the defense industry, they neglected to mention the enforcement provision failings of Executive Order 8802. The newspapers and black leaders who jumped on the FDR bandwagon apparently decided that maybe Democrats, who all along had been in favor of lynching black people, were not *really* that bad after all. Blacks began to abandon the Republican Party.

MORE MEDIA GENERATED FOLKLORE:

"DEMOCRAT HARRY TRUMAN VOLUNTARILY TOOK THE HIGH ROAD AND DESEGREGATED THE ARMED FORCES."

Black Americans have always been patriotic. They have fought and died in all the wars fought by the American military from the Revolution to Operation Iraqi Freedom. In earlier conflicts, they served as combat troops, but in WWII, while some did see combat, their service was primarily limited to support roles and menial tasks. Nevertheless, on their return they brought with them a new set of expectations. They had not been satisfied with their status in the military; they had experienced new freedoms in the liberated European theater. Things would have to change.

In the mid 1940s, America found herself engaged in a Cold War. The Soviet Union's expansionist ideology helped precipitate a head-on collision of the past and the future of Black's civil rights. Communism was on the move everywhere, and America was occupied in a police action in North Korea. The rapid demobilization of the armed forces at the end of the WWII had to be reversed. To quickly rebuild the military, President Truman reinstated the draft. Enter A. Philip Randolph (remember him?) and Grant Reynolds, former military chaplain, now Commissioner of Corrections for New York State. Randolph, Reynolds, and three other African-American leaders were invited to meet with President Truman to discuss segregation in the military:

"As Randolph remembers, the meeting had been proceeding smoothly and amicably, until he said to Truman, 'Mr. President, after making several trips around the country, I can tell you that the mood among Negroes of this country is that they will never bear arms again until all forms of bias and discrimination are abolished.'

"In a battle of bluntness Harry Truman came out second to no man, and he told Randolph, 'I wish you hadn't made that statement. I don't like it at all.

"Charles Houston intervened: 'But Mr. President, don't you want to know what is happening in the country?' Truman said he certainly wanted to know what was happening in the country; a president attracted more than enough yes men.

"'Well, that's what I'm giving you, Mr. President,' Randolph said, seizing the advantage before it disappeared again. 'I'm giving you the facts.' When the President allowed him to proceed,

Randolph ran headlong into Truman again: 'Mr. President, as you know, we are calling upon you to issue an executive order abolishing segregation in the armed forces.' At this point, Truman simply thanked his visitors for coming, and said there didn't seem to be much more that they could talk fruitfully about.

"But Truman's rebuff merely aroused Randolph's defiance. Testifying, nine days later, during hearings on the universal military training bill, Randolph told the Senate Armed Services Committee:

"'This time Negroes will not take a Jim Crow draft lying down. The conscience of the world will be shaken as by nothing else when thousands and thousands of us second-class Americans choose imprisonment in preference to permanent military slavery...I personally will advise Negroes to refuse to fight as slaves for a democracy they cannot possess and cannot enjoy."'[3]

Once again a Democrat president found himself in the crosshairs. Blacks were not going to be drafted and sent to fight and die in a war to secure for others liberties *they* did not themselves possess; they would boycott the draft. Black men would engage in massive civil disobedience by refusing to register for, or obey, the draft. One can easily visualize the social and civil ramifications of such an act; plus, Blacks were sorely needed in the new buildup. President Truman "took the high road" and issued Executive Order 9981. The U.S. military was desegregated.

When I joined the Air Force in 1955, they were still working out the kinks. Three years after basic training and technical school, I met several white members of my former basic training troop, and although I was in a more advanced technical field, they all outranked me by several stripes. Yes, there was still discrimination, albeit covert, but it was there nonetheless. (See author's book, *Plain Bread*, www.benkinchlow.com)

CHAPTER 10

PARTY ON, DUDE!

WHY I LIKE IKE

It was September 1957, and I was a long way from Uvalde, Texas. Sidi Slimane Air Base, in French Morocco, was on alert again. We were pulling armed guard duty around the flight line, because SAC (Strategic Air Command) B-47 Bombers were stationed there. Everyone heard the rumors of riots and uprisings by the Moroccans, and scuttlebutt had it that there had been several attempts at sabotage on the flight line. We were all working 12 on 12 off. Everybody was jumpy. I had finished my 12 on and was just walking into the barracks lounge. The TV was on and AFRTS (Armed Forces Radio and Television Services News) was showing The 101st Airborne Division on point, weapons at the ready. One of America's elite fighting units, the Screaming Eagles, was arrayed in front of a building with bayonets fixed (fixed bayonets are serious). WAR! "Russia has invaded the Unites States!" was my first thought.

"Hey, turn it up, looks like an invasion or something back home!" I grabbed a chair and perched on the edge, my half-empty lukewarm Pepsi all but forgotten. We all focused on the TV. Crowds had gathered, and we could tell the folks back home were not happy. In fact, they were enraged, yelling, and screaming, their faces contorted. "It *must* be an attack! Why else would Americans be so angry?" We could hear an announcer, "They are approaching, and U.S. Marshals are surrounding them!" Federal Marshals protecting Russians? It was deathly still in the day-room. We may have halfway expected a war to break out, but not at *home!* Isn't that why we were *here*, to prevent anything from happening back *there*? The camera was swinging around to focus on the enemy. "What's going on?" A chorus of "ssshhhh" silenced the questioner; the enemy was coming into view.

"What the …?!" Two black teenage girls, one in a white dress, followed by seven other black teens (three boys and four girls), protected by the fixed bayonets of one thousand members of the 101st Airborne Division and eight federal marshals, marched with their heads up past jeering students, angry mothers, and raging Klansmen into an American high school. Central High School, Little Rock, Arkansas, USA - under the bayonets of the 101st Airborne, fixed on exactly the kind of rifle I'd just turned in that morning - had been integrated.

Unknown to most Blacks, the Republican Party facilitated most of the civil rights gains of the '60s. In 1957, Congress passed the first Civil Rights Act since Reconstruction. Signed by President Dwight D. Eisenhower in September, it established the Civil Rights Division at the Department of Justice, headed by an assistant attorney general who would enforce federal statutes that dealt with civil rights and investigate complaints.

The Eisenhower Administration sent federal election officials to protect black voters, federalized the National Guard, and sent U.S. troops to Little Rock. President Eisenhower was the first president since Reconstruction, and only the second president in history, to use federal troops to support African-American rights. Some claim he did it reluctantly to enforce national sovereignty, not integration; but the fact remains, he did it — and America is the better for it.

Since Reconstruction, southern Democrats had demanded all federal programs be controlled at the local level, insisted on states' rights and a hands-off policy on matters of race. Let me remind all - seniority equals power in Congress, and southern Democrats were re-elected time after time. They controlled the major committee chairs, sat on the most powerful committees, and held out the constant threat of filibuster, where a few southern senators could block almost any legislation, civil rights or otherwise. No president could risk alienating the powerful southern wing of the party. They controlled the Congress and legislation.

Throughout the 1950s, civil rights groups had lobbied the federal government for fair housing legislation, but southern Democrats blocked every effort. Two years into his presidency, and only after the NAACP had flooded the White House with ballpoint pens in a letter-writing campaign, President Kennedy signed Executive Order 11063, fulfilling his promise to "act swiftly" on discrimination in federal housing. The signing, however, was largely symbolic. It was not until after the King assassination and subsequent riots that Congress passed The Fair Housing Act of 1968.[1] Let the record show, no Democrat president or Democrat controlled Congress from 1875 to 1965, including JFK, has, absent political or public pressure, *voluntarily* initiated any meaningful civil rights legislation for African-Americans.

PARTY ON, DUDE!

Since the '60s, the black vote has had an impact on both parties; positive for the Democrats, and negative for Republicans. The strategy for the Republican Party has been to pick up a few votes in the black community and neutralize the rest by a large turnout among white voters. If a party can make significant inroads into the Hispanic community, they will begin to question the necessity of making even token overtures to the Black community. "After all," the argument will run, "No matter what we do, they are going to vote Democrat," and Democrats will, as they have in the past, take the black vote for granted, based on promises of "Mo Money, Mo Money."

With a leadership that consistently positions black concerns on the leftist fringe of the American political spectrum, Blacks risk being written off as a disaffected mob. "No matter what you do, you can't please 'em." Once politicians have made the obligatory tip of the tam, all bets are off. For African-Americans, this could bring about a serious political crisis - becoming marginalized. Politicians focus on those groups that offer their party the potential for the greatest return on any investment of money, time, and political capital. At one point, Blacks, as the largest minority bloc, were the "swing" vote. Blacks no longer have that distinction. Hispanics, now the largest minority, are growing in numbers and influence.

MR. AND MRS. BLACK CONSERVATIVE

For decades, African-Americans have consistently voted the party line and black leaders have apparently deliberately hidden, or made little effort to ascertain the historical facts. The truly ironic part of this political dance is that Blacks have traditionally danced with a partner with whom they have little in common. By today's political standards, most Blacks would be considered right wing conservatives, not left wing liberals for whom they vote: [2]

ISSUE	BLACKS SUPPORT	REPS SUPPORT	DEMS OPPOSE
School Prayer	80%	✓	X
Education Vouchers	73%	✓	X
Faith-Based Initiatives	74%	✓	X
English as Official Language	84%	✓	X
Death Penalty	64%	✓	X

ISSUE	BLACKS OPPOSE	REPS OPPOSE	DEMS SUPPORT
Race-based preferences (Affirmative Action)	86%	X	✓
Legalization of Pot	75%	X	✓
Same-Sex Marriage	71%	X	✓

Clearly, Democrats and Blacks are on different pages when it comes to basic values. So let me get this straight; Blacks **embrace** conservative values, but **vote** liberal values. The obvious question then is — what can be done about it?

CHAPTER 11

VIRTUAL RACISM

WHAT DO?

An intelligent, articulate lady who writes poetry, paints, and prays for me regularly had an unusual call-to-action. When her three teenage daughters would approach her with a problem, she would begin her solution with, "Okay, here's what do..." If the leaders of our country, with a heart for America, were open to suggestions on how to encourage African-Americans to participate in our Republic as proactive, not reactive, voters, I would begin with, "Here's what do!"

FIRST: Despite the wails of the leftist-oriented media, and the self-serving assertions of their media-anointed *civil rights leaders*, recognize and act on these simple truths: *all white Americans are not racists, and all Blacks are not victims.* Most Americans, in fact, the *overwhelming* majority of Americans, black or white, do not spend every waking hour fixated on race. If the truth be known, most are fed up with hearing almost every problem couched in racial terms. If I were a betting man, I would give odds that in most cases, when the race issue is brought up, it is in, or in response to, some news story.

SECOND: Americans, as a general rule, are too busy making a living, rooting for their favorite sports team, negotiating government red tape, or trying to avoid being taxed into poverty to spend hours absorbed in racial drama.

THIRD: Most Whites are tired of being blamed for something they had nothing to do with ~ slavery. Most Blacks are not sitting around looking for some white person to blame ~ for slavery. If Americans were permitted by the Politically Correct Thought Police (PCTP) to express what they really feel, I am convinced the vast majority would say, "Enough with the race stuff already, let's get on with it!"

FINALLY: America is the least racist, most accepting of culture and class of any country on the face of the earth. (Been to Bosnia, Africa, or the Middle East lately? And the French don't like *anybody* very much.) Civil rights leaders relentlessly proclaim that America is rife with racism, and all manner of supposed malevolence is brought fourth in support of these charges. Yet, just let *almost* any public figure be tarred with what the majority of white Americans consider racism, and "Good-bye Charlie." Ask Trent Lott and Don Imus of recent "mis-speak" fame. When a Republican bureaucrat used "niggardly" to describe the size of a budget allocation (as if the word had *anything* to do with the commonly accepted use of the "N" word), he was forced to resign. However it seems this standard does not necessarily apply to Democrats or liberals. Compare the tribute Senator Dodd gave Senator Byrd on the floor of the U.S. Senate with the remarks made by Senator Lott about Thurmond at a private party:

<u>Sen. Christopher Dodd</u>: (Congressional Record)

"I do not think it is an exaggeration at all to say to my friend from West Virginia that he would have been a great senator at any moment." "Some were right for the time. Robert C. Byrd, in my view, would have been right at any time." Dodd continued, the West Virginia Democrat *"would have been right at the founding of this country, right during the Civil War."* And concluded, *"I cannot think of a single moment in this nation's 220-plus year history where [Byrd] would not have been a valuable asset to this country."*

<u>Senator Trent Lott</u>: (C-Span)

"I want to say this about my state - When Strom Thurmond ran for president, we voted for him. We're proud of it. And if the rest of the country had followed our lead, we wouldn't have had all these problems over all these years."

It is interesting, at least to me, that critics, especially black critics, managed to selectively excerpt the history of both men when complimenting or castigating. Senator Byrd's former Klan activities were completely overlooked. The senior senator from West Virginia (President Pro Tempore; immediately behind the Speaker of the House in the line of presidential succession; formerly a Grand Kleagle and Exalted Cyclops in the KKK; nicknamed "Sheets" by House Speaker Tip O'Neill) once vowed he would, *"...never fight with a Negro by my side, Rather I should die a thousand times, and see Old Glory trampled in the dirt never to rise again, than to see this beloved land of ours become degraded by race mongrels, a throwback to the blackest specimen from the wilds."* [1]

This same "highly respected conscience of the Senate" deliberately used the "N" word twice on national TV (FOX News). *"There are white niggers. I've seen a lot of white niggers in my time; I'm going to use that word."* The thunderous silence from the black political leaders and leftist pundits, who would later castigate Senator Lott and Don Imus, was deafening. Equally hidden from our erstwhile eagle-eyed critics was this 1997 article in the *Charlotte Observer* about the integration of the University of Mississippi when Lott was a student cheerleader there:

> *"On Sunday night,* [black student, James] *Meredith came to campus,"* the paper reported. *"A mob, including many non-students, bombarded marshals with bricks and bottles. Student leaders — including Trent Lott, now U.S. Senate majority leader — tried to discourage violence, but a riot broke out."*

Note to the PCTP (Politically Correct Thought Police): No defense of Lott's right to 1st Amendment speech is intended or implied. I am fully aware that the Founding Fathers intended that privilege for the Left only. Let there be equal opportunity criticism. If one tribute should be criticized, so should the other.

It should be noted; the use of the adjective "black" can be confusing to some. For example, William Jefferson Clinton was "our first black president." This bouquet was bestowed apparently in recognition of some *constructive approach and beneficial contribution* to race relations. Facts, it seems, should not be considered when bouquets are bestowed; facts confuse the issue. For example, the NAACP sued the then apparently more-white-than-black Gov. Clinton in 1989 for violating the federal Voting Rights Act of 1965. A three-judge panel in Arkansas ordered him to redraw electoral districts to allow Blacks greater voting strength. Perhaps his being

"Our First Black President" explains why the *black leadership* ignored his remarks at a presentation of America's highest honor for civilians, the Presidential Medal of Freedom, on May 5, 1993: at a "*...moving 88th birthday ceremony for former Senator William Fulbright, President Clinton last night bestowed the Presidential Medal of Freedom on the man he described as a visionary humanitarian, a steadfast supporter of the values of education, and 'my mentor.'*" Clinton added, "*It doesn't take long to live a life. He made the best of his, and helped us to have a better chance to make the best of ours...The American political system produced this remarkable man, and my state did, and I'm real proud of it.*" [2]

"Values of education" is an interesting choice of words, considering Senator Fulbright signed a 1954 "Southern Manifesto" denouncing the *Brown vs. Board of Education* and stating, among other things, "*We commend the motives of those states which have declared the intention to resist forced integration by any lawful means...*" The "remarkable man" also voted against the 1964 Civil Rights Bill and the 1965 Voting Rights Act. President Clinton was "real proud" that America had produced this rabid segregationist, his "mentor."

Guess whom the Black Prez did not care about offending when, as governor in April 1985, he signed into law Act 985, combining into a state holiday on the same day the birth dates of Martin Luther King Jr. and Gen. Robert E. Lee? I am still waiting for the black "Freedom Fighters" and the "Civil Rights Leaders" (who all just happen to be Democrats) to raise the chorus of condemnation to at least half the decibel level of that for Lott, Imus, and the un-mourned Republican bureaucrat. How do you spell "Hy-po-crite?"

WHAT I MEANT WAS...

In a speech to the NAACP, and another to the National Urban League, Vice President Al Gore, who garnered 90% of the black vote in 2000, was heard to say words to the effect that his father lost his Senate seat because he supported civil rights legislation. According to the Congressional Quarterly, Al Gore *Sr.,* along with all southern Democrats, voted *against* the Civil Rights Act of 1964. Moreover, Senator Gore did not simply vote against it, he sent the bill to the Senate Judiciary Committee with an amendment saying, *"in defiance of a court desegregation order, federal funds could not be held from any school districts."* In other words, just in case the 1964 Civil Rights Act did pass, federal funds could not be held back from schools refusing to end segregation. (The Amendment was defeated 74-25.) The moral of the story is, as a member of the elitist left, you don't have to stick to the facts; if history doesn't suit, alter it.

As a revolutionary nicknamed *Malcolm Z* in the Black Liberation Front (the more militant wing of the Civil Rights movement in the '60s), I learned one of the basic tactics in use today - Racial Rhetoric 101... fight facts with fertilizer, history with histrionics, and when all else fails, bring out the name calling; "Honky," "Cracker," and the old standby, "Racist" work best on "Whitey." (Avoid "redneck" – it's been favorably co-opted. See Introduction for extensive list of putdowns for Blacks). "Racist" can be used quite effectively as a modifier for *pig, dog, conservatives, Republicans, bankers, homophobes,* etc., etc., ad nauseum. For effect, this is best done with a slight curl of the upper left side of the top lip. Dreadlocks, or a shaved head with a Fu Manchu mustache, maximize impact. (Afros are passé).

VIRTUAL RACISM

It seems to me that if White America were as racist as many critics allege, *racist* would be a label eagerly sought by politicians and other public figures. In my opinion, much of what is presently being investigated, inveighed, and legislated against is what I call *"virtual racism."* As someone who has personally experienced the institutionalized segregation and hard-core racism of the '40s, '50s, and '60s, not the "virtual racism" of today, I am mystified at the seeming dichotomy in some of the charges. This *virtual* racism causing black leaders such heartburn today would have once been hailed by the rank and file Blacks as having reached the Promised Land. In the '40s, '50s, or even the '60s, the prospect of having been *possibly* redlined for a loan, *perhaps* not promoted on a well-paying job with a major corporation, to have encountered an *insensitive* clerk in a major department store, or experienced *deliberately slow service* in a restaurant chain would have been an occasion for singing *"We have overcome..."*

With all due respect to any potential irregularities that may have occurred during the 2000 presidential election, to claim a whole race of people is "disenfranchised" because some few people (black and white) in several predominately Democrat controlled precincts in Florida did not know how to punch the equivalent of a Bingo card is, to my mind, a bit over the top.

In my opinion (I am still entitled to my own?), this *virtual racism* is like *virtual football* or a *virtual war game.* You can get quite exercised about it, but it's not likely to draw blood. Civil rights demonstrations today mostly consist of black and white liberal students harassing black or white conservative students or speakers at Ivy League schools where black students demand (and get) "Ujamaa Houses" (separate black dorms and eating facilities). Yo, Dudes, I hate to bring this up, but we *had* separate dorms, separate eating facilities – all that and *much more*. We also didn't have to insist on "white folk" not intruding into our *cultural space*. If memory serves, we fought to *get **out of*** not ***into*** segregated dormitories and eating facilities.

Back in the day, there was bonafide (not *virtual*) racism - with police dogs, billy clubs, water cannons (high pressure fire hoses that could take off real skin), lynchings, and bombs killing little black girls in church. I well recall the response of a certain southern governor when charged with being a segregationist, "Yes!" he thundered, pulling himself up to his full five feet some-odd inches, "Segregation today, segregation tomorrow, and segregation forever!" Denigrated, spat upon, last hired-first fired, denied basic human rights (much less civil rights), black people "back in the day" understood who racists were and what racism really meant. The civil rights movement, the sit-ins, the marches, the Freedom Riders, and their deaths were sparked as much by the lynching of Emmett Till, a young Black from Chicago, as by Rosa Parks' refusal to relinquish her seat in the segregated section on a bus in Montgomery, Alabama.

Here is a quick refresher course for those "stressed out" Blacks in a predominately white school who may feel a bit put upon or discriminated against by *virtual* racism. According to the National Park Service, students at Little Rock High School were elbowed, poked, kicked, punched, and pushed; faced verbal abuse from segregationists, as well as death threats against themselves, their families, and members of the black community. At home, their families received threatening phone calls; some of the parents lost their jobs; and the black community as a whole was harassed by bomb threats, gunshots, and bricks thrown through windows. The students were also alienated by those [Blacks] who felt their actions jeopardized the safety of others. One of the Little Rock Nine, Melba Pattillo Beals, was stabbed and had acid (which could have blinded her) thrown in her face.

She describes their experience in her book *Warriors Don't Cry:*[3]

"My eight friends and I paid for the integration of Central High with our innocence. During those years when we desperately needed approval from our peers, we were victims of the most harsh rejection imaginable. The physical and psychological punishment we endured profoundly affected our lives. It transformed us into warriors who dared not cry even when we suffered intolerable pain."

Off-hand, I'd say times have changed.

SO WHO IS THIS JAMES "JIM" CROW?

Jim Crow is a phrase taken from a song of the same name and later minstrel shows portraying Blacks as buffoons, clowns and idiots. Finally it became an epithet, leading to and supporting the implementation of a legal system known as "Jim Crow."

At the risk of offending, and perhaps being redundant or worse, being relegated to a bygone era, let me just offer an extremely brief refresher course on some *actual*, not *virtual*, racist policies:

The Blind:

Maintain a separate building...on separate ground for the admission, care, instruction, and support of all blind persons of the colored or black race. (Louisiana)

Education:

Separate schools shall be maintained for the children of the white and colored races. (Mississippi)

Textbooks:

Books shall not be interchangeable between the white and colored schools. (North Carolina)

Telephone Booths:

Maintain separate booths for white and colored patrons (Oklahoma)

Lunch Counters:

No persons, firms, or corporations, who or which furnish meals to passengers at station restaurants or station eating hous-es ...shall furnish said meals to white and colored passengers in the same room, or at the same table, or at the same counter. (South Carolina)

Juvenile Delinquents:

Separate buildings, not nearer than one-fourth mile to each other, one for white boys and one for Negro boys. (Florida)

Mental Hospitals:

Distinct apartments are arranged for said patients, so that in no case shall Negroes and white persons be together. (Georgia)

Intermarriage:

It shall be unlawful for a white person to marry anyone except a white person. Any marriage in violation of this section shall be void. (Georgia)

Amateur Baseball:

Unlawful for any amateur white baseball team to play baseball on any vacant lot or baseball diamond within two blocks of a playground devoted to the Negro race, and it shall be unlawful for any amateur colored baseball team to play baseball in any vacant lot or baseball diamond within two blocks of any playground devoted to the white race. (Georgia)

Parks:

Unlawful for colored people to frequent any park owned or maintained by the city for the benefit, use, and enjoyment of white persons.... (Georgia)

And one final indignity...

Burial:

Shall not bury, or allow to be buried, any colored persons upon ground set apart or used for the burial of white persons. (Georgia)

So, what *about* heaven? All the representations of Jesus portray Him as white. Is there any hope for black folks to get through the pearly gates and walk the streets of gold? Fortunately, there does appear to be *some* hope. I met a staunch, dyed-in-the-wool Southern Baptist deacon who had the ultimate solution to that problem. As co-host of *The 700 Club*, a popular national and internationally televised Christian talk show, there existed a common assumption among Whites and Blacks who watched that I was surely a prime candidate for heaven. When this white Christian gentleman was asked, in my presence, whether Blacks like "Brother Ben" could make it to heaven, he said warmly and sincerely, "Of course! "When we get there, we'll all be whiter than snow." True story.

CHAPTER 12

THEN IT WAS "SEGREGATION" ~ NOW IT'S "DIVERSITY"

PICK A LABEL, ANY LABEL

I have been alternately Colored, Negro, Afro-American, and Black. A word of explanation, at this point, may be helpful to the white Americans reading this. If the way "Black" or "black" is thrown around seems a bit confusing, it is to black folks as well. It all depends on how and when you use *Black* or *black*. "Black" can be pejorative or salutary depending on its use. I could call someone a vile epithet without consequence, but if I prefaced it with "black," it was an invitation to a fight. Then it became "Say it loud... I'm Black and I'm proud." As of this writing, I am officially classified as an African-American. But, I have a white friend who was born in South Africa, and is now an American citizen. Is he an African-American?

I have a question regarding "cultural diversity." What exactly does that mean?

Some of America's finest universities are now insisting "diversity education" requires the admission of Blacks (or is that "blacks") to insure that "white" (or is that White) students are exposed to "black ideas." "Black Ideas?" Are Blacks *that* different - simply because they are *Black?* Do Blacks have some sort of peculiar mindset so genetically indigenous as to be totally alien to/from the plain old vanilla white kids on the Yale, Harvard, or MIT campuses? Does black ethnicity require a forced diversity to prepare white students for life? Radical black and white liberal professors, diversity politics, the hip-hop culture, mainstream black TV programs, and movies all convey the image of Blacks as being somehow different. Whites cannot be blamed if they wonder *"Who are Black people? What do they want?"* The average white person knows what the average white person wants; but ask the average white person what the average black person wants, and you will most likely hear the average answer..."*I don't know.*"

No one person can speak for all Blacks. I certainly do not pretend or aspire to, but I can tell you this - most Blacks do not want to be selected just because they are **black**. They just do not want to be **not** selected just because they **are** black!

TAKE ME, PLEASE!

Take me, for example. I am dark, but physically I am not black. I am not as dark as some Blacks, and some Blacks are white enough to (and do) "pass." American Blacks are not consistently as dark as African Blacks, unless, of course, the African

Blacks are Colored Blacks who are not as dark as the African *black* Blacks. Got it? No? OK... again. American Blacks...

What about my friend Armando? How different is he because he is Hispanic? Is my friend Bob, a Wall Street guru, that different just because he is a "WASNDP" (White Anglo-Saxon Non-Denominational Protestant)? What of my friend Keith, a WASCC? (White Anglo-Saxon Charismatic Catholic) or my friend Chris, a WASA (White Anglo-Saxon Agnostic)? And, oh yes, my friend Earl, the token WASP (White Anglo-Saxon Protestant)?

By the way, what is the politically correct term for "Whites" now - racists?

Race is a 21st century fact of life. Liberals, the media elite, and the so-called *black leadership* have made it so. There is no escaping this. Liberals, *black leaders*, and media pundits employ the race card to make points against conservatives, against each other, and anyone else bold enough to disagree with them.

KEEPING IT REAL

Let <u>me</u> play a race card. With the possible exception of the original "Cosby Show," Blacks were, as a whole, seldom, if ever, portrayed as mainstream. I recall the controversy just prior to the Cosby Show going off the air. Dr. Cliff Huxtable, M.D., and his attorney wife, Claire, did not (according to the liberal black intelligentsia) *accurately portray the black experience.* Shows portraying Blacks as entertainers, sports stars, ghetto dwellers, and/or buffoons escaped unscathed; they fit the *profile.* With all due respect to Mr. Cosby, and Ms. Rashad, even the marvelous chemistry between them was not sufficient to propel his comeback attempt (at realism) back into the double-digit ratings they once enjoyed. The audience for the original Cosby Show flocked *away* from this more *realistic* portrayal of the Black experience.

Few would seriously attempt to deny that some forms of racism, elitism, and prejudice do exist. However, the simple fact is, as a general rule, people tend to associate with those with whom they feel comfortable and abandon their comfort zones only under duress. "Birds of a feather…" people attend churches, nightclubs, restaurants, concerts, or operas where the people (whatever color they are) act "right." Loosely translated, *acting right* means *they act like me or in a manner acceptable to me*. As a general rule, most people are not comfortable in unfamiliar surroundings so they avoid them.

In the spirit of keeping it real, let's break this thing down further. In the '60s, I was a Black Muslim, a militant, a revolutionary - albeit a *moderate* revolutionary. My position was, "Let's negotiate with Whitey; if he doesn't accede to our demands, let's blow him up." My younger brother, fed up with what he perceived as our slow progress, became a *radical* revolutionary. His position was "Let's blow them up; then negotiate with the survivors." This made some Whites nervous. This made some *Blacks* nervous. There were black people who did not feel comfortable around people like us. Just as there are Whites that do not associate with, or feel comfortable around, skinheads, there are Blacks that do not embrace or associate with "gangstas." Many people may experience some uneasiness when encountering a group of young males with bandanas or shaved heads, big unlaced yellow work boots, tattoos, super baggy pants, and oversized shirts or undershirts. And who can forget Jesse Jackson's inadvertent admission, *"There is nothing more painful to me at this stage in my life than to walk down the street and hear foot-*

steps and start thinking about robbery...then look around, see some-body White, and feel relieved."

Heated rhetoric from self-appointed or media-elected critics to the contrary, Blacks and Whites in America get along much better than Protestants and Catholics in Ireland; Chinese and Tibetans, Muslims and Kurds; Muslims and *Muslims* (Shiite and Suni); Indians and Pakistanis; or Hutu and Tutsi, etc., etc., ad nauseum. Here is one tragic example of selective criticism: In Burundi, not too long ago, 150,000 Blacks were ruthlessly slaughtered by other Blacks in less than seven years (including 300 women and children in one day). Where were the cries of outrage from national and/or international black leaders? Where were the demands for UN military intervention and/or reparations? I suppose they were busy pondering the modern (as in today) slave trade in Africa where Muslims (who are black) are capturing, kidnapping, and selling Christians (also black) into slavery. Perhaps they are mulling over the fact that the overwhelming incidence of crime in the black community here in America is Black on Black crime. Thankfully, leftists (black and white) still have the white male (the last real minority) driving out to suburban neighborhoods in his "gas guzzling" SUV to blame; otherwise, black folk might have to accept some respon-sibility for some of those activities.

APPLES AND AFFIRMATIVE ACTION

Most government programs endorsed or sponsored by lib-erals have not only failed miserably but have done significant damage to the black family.

First, let me clear up a common misunderstanding. African-Americans are not a monolithic group politically, economically, or socially. Analysts and pundits who classify them as such inadvertently or deliberately misinform their target audience and propose misguided solutions. Part of the problem for all Americans is that racial/liberal demagogues refuse to allow reasoned discourse when race is involved. Every discussion on race is held at deafening decibel levels and peppered (dare I say it?) **liberally** with *racially insensitive* labeling. Any hint of the eminently provable charge that welfare doesn't work is hooted down as *bigoted*. The same fate awaits anyone, black or white, who dares touch another sacred cow of academia...*Affirmative Action*. Courts have ruled that *race can be a factor* in deciding who should be admitted. Isn't that precisely what kept *my* generation out of public schools? Hmmm.

Generally speaking, most liberals (and their surrogates in politics) focus on roughly 20% of the African-American population. Affirmative Action primarily helps the *elite* 5%, and the various public assistance programs target *the underprivileged* 15%. (By the way, what exactly does *the underprivileged* mean in a free republic? Is that the opposite of *the privileged?* The equivalent of the *untouchables* in India?) The whole idea of a republic, a democratic form of government, was to erase the concept of the "privileged" class (i.e., the Royals) and the "underprivileged" (the peasants). In America, contrary to the new "victimology," class does not limit opportunity. There are countless instances of people in this country who have succeeded magnificently against all odds. America **is** the land of opportunity.

What about Affirmative Action? Do Blacks, as liberals and black *spokesmen* adamantly affirm, overwhelmingly support the concept of affirmative action? Let us review the original intent of affirmative action - then determine whether or not the majority of African-Americans support it.

The first official use of the phrase "affirmative action" was by John F. Kennedy in Executive Order 10925 *addressing discrimination in government contracts*. This executive order required the federal government to take *affirmative action* to ensure there was no discrimination in employment and hiring practices in projects funded by the U.S. government. Though on the books, it only requested voluntary compliance and that was not strictly enforced. In 1965, President Lyndon B. Johnson followed up with Executive Order 11246, again requiring firms doing business under government contracts to take "affirmative action" in considering minority employment. Contractors were required to document the fact that they were in compliance. In 1967, gender was added; but, again, no *requirements for action* were set. Although initially introduced by JFK and restated by LBJ, no actual concrete steps were taken until President Richard Nixon introduced the "Philadelphia Order" - conceived, crafted, and implemented by a black Republican, Assistant Secretary of Labor, Dr. Arthur A. Fletcher. This plan contained "goals and timetables, not quotas." It also went a step further and required withholding funds from contractors who failed to comply with these requirements.[1]

The *original intent* of affirmative action has changed, as illustrated by the case of Bakke vs. University of California Regents and the University of Michigan Law School's affirmative action policy. In 1978, Allan Bakke, a 35-year old white student, applied to University of California's Davis Medical School. He was rejected and his slot given to a minority applicant who was selected despite having lower scores. He applied again and was rejected again. This time Bakke sued, claiming he was denied equal protection under the 14th Amendment, and won. The school could not discriminate against him in favor of a minority.

In the University of Michigan Law School case however, a federal judge ruled, in effect, that the use of race as a factor in admissions *is* "Constitutional." Clearly, judicial activists, left-leaning politicians, and liberal educators have dramatically altered the intent of affirmative action. Originally designed to prevent discrimination against minorities in government funded projects, Affirmative Action has become the driving force behind a social re-engineering movement. This new movement allows race to be used again as a determinant and will inevitably lead to hatred, hostility, and violence.

The question is - do Blacks overwhelmingly support the current concept of Affirmative Action? When asked, *"In order to give minorities more opportunity, do you believe race or ethnicity should be a factor when deciding who is hired, promoted, or admitted to college, or that hiring, promotions, and college admissions should be based strictly on merit and qualifications other than race or ethnicity?"* 86% of the African-American population gave the following response: [It] **"Should be based strictly on merit and qualifications *other* than race/ethnicity."**[2] Sixty-nine percent of Blacks rejected the following statement: *"To make up for past discrimination, women and members of minority groups should be given preferential treatment getting jobs and placement in college."* They chose instead; **"Ability, as determined by test scores, should be the main consideration."** Furthermore, 90% of Blacks rejected "admitting a black applicant over a white applicant with SAT scores 25 points higher." (1991 Gallup Poll)

The facts suggest that 80% of African-Americans, in fact, *most* Americans, do not actually benefit from these programs; and Americans, as a whole, reject the idea of preferential treatment based on race or ethnicity. In other words, *properly polled*, Blacks, by a large margin, oppose race-based preferences. They are *not* looking to be adopted as wards of federal, state, or local governments.

The less than enthusiastic acceptance of government set-asides by the general population is based on a desire to see that all Americans have the opportunity to succeed. The majority of Americans support opportunity and question these giveaway programs. They tolerate them, motivated by a sense of fair play, but what Americans really love is challenge and competition. America's national motto could very well be, "May the best man win!" As with almost all Americans, the guidelines most Blacks would choose to live by are: *impartiality*, *fair play*, and a *level playing field*.

"MONEY! MONEY! MONEY! MONEY!"
~ The O'Jays

Is there a solution? A broad-based, multi-faceted approach that could work across the board? A resounding YES!! And the solution is not just "Mo Money." First, recognize a fifteen trillion dollar truth (the amount spent to date since LBJ's *Great Society* was launched): *Ongoing charity as a solution to a problem simply does not work. Long-term charity produces negative side effects and should never be entered into as a permanent solution.*

Liberals have now cast welfare as an *entitlement*; something a citizen has a "right" to. Something as destructive to both the individual and society as welfare should not be positioned as something one is entitled to. Welfare destroys personal initiative, promotes apathy, generates dependency, and is resented by the donor as well as the recipient. Taxpayers hate high tax rates and welfare recipients hate being objects of pity. What *most* Americans of all backgrounds want is an opportunity to compete equally. America is still the land of opportunity.

The primary argument in favor of Affirmative Action, as it is presently interpreted, is based on the leftist liberal argument that institutionalized racism has produced inferior Blacks and superior Whites. Blacks, they insist, require an advantage in order to compete with the "superior counterparts" of other ethnic groups.

These questions are seldom, if ever, addressed: How did Blacks achieve prior to Affirmative Action? Have any achieved without Affirmative Action or other government assistance? The inference is that only Blacks, as opposed to Whites, Orientals, or practically any other immigrant group, inherently lack the capacity to achieve without government assistance. Almost all intelligent, successful, self-motivated black Americans are insulted by the innate plantation mentality of this type of program. This was precisely the argument put forth in the '40s and '50s to justify segregation. We were told, "Segregation is for your benefit; since you are unable to compete intellectually or academically with superior white students, you must have your own schools." Then they called it "separate but equal," now they call it Affirmative Action.

Affirmative Action, objectively viewed, is simply racial profiling, as the following example of Orwellian doublespeak clearly illustrates: Singling out a young black male on the New Jersey Turnpike because he is a young black male is <u>racial profiling</u>. Singling out that <u>same</u> young black male on the Rutgers campus (also in New Jersey), because he is a young black male, is <u>Affirmative Action</u>. The end result is a plantation mentality, a new form of slavery – new generations of Blacks dependent upon subsidies from "the big white house." I know of fourth-generation recipients of these government entitlements, and only a radical shift in the thought process prevented the continuation into the fifth and sixth generations.

Many of the "assistance" programs introduced and supported by Democrats, liberals, and the un-elected Black leadership ultimately appear to be anti-black in their orientation. Thomas Sowell, a respected African-American economist with the Hoover Institution at Stanford University, gives us the following perspective on government assistance:

> "The assumption that spending more of the taxpayer's money will make things better has survived all kinds of evidence that it has made things worse. The black family — which survived slavery, discrimination, poverty, wars and depressions — began to come apart as the federal government moved in with its well-financed programs to 'help.'"

By every measure, his assessment has proven accurate. To paraphrase Dr. Sowell, *"The Black family has survived everything except government help."*

"IF STUPIDITY GOT US INTO THIS MESS, THEN WHY CAN'T IT GET US OUT?"

~ Will Rogers

The borrower is the servant of the lender. (Proverbs 22:7) The "man" that controls your money controls you. Democrats and their liberal allies are aware of this and are determined to keep Blacks dependent, because they know those who rely on any kind of support mechanism will do nothing to jeopardize that relationship. It's called *plantation politics.* "Massa" is no longer in a big white building in Mississippi, but a big white building in Washington DC.

What African-Americans don't *need* is exactly what the liberals are trying to give ~ another government program. Entitlement programs have had a severe impact on the stability of the Black family. There have been dramatic increases in:

- Illegitimate births
- "Head of Household" single mothers
- Absentee fathers
- Numbers at poverty level
- Incidents of Black on Black crime
- Black prison populations
- Dependence on government subsidies
- Lack of initiative and self-reliance

TALK TO ME SO YOU CAN SEE
WHAT'S GOING ON
~ Marvin Gaye

In the years since Goldwater, one of the main reasons Republicans have remained on the defensive in the African-American community is because they are portrayed as *insensitive.* For years GOP spokesmen were always white, so Democrats, with token black spokesman, were able to stay on the offensive with the ubiquitous cry of "Racism!" The character assassins on the left, like good Marxist propagandists, trotted out the racist tag on cue. When epithets are used, reason is not.

If Republican progress is to be seen in the black community, they, as did Democrats after Reconstruction, must initiate a definitive change in strategy. Here are a few suggested steps that can be implemented with a minimum of restructuring or financing. In order to communicate effectively to the black community, Republicans should immediately begin to:

- Disregard the conventional wisdom espoused by the liberal press

- Recognize the un-elected black leadership is not representative of grassroots black America

- Focus on the 80% of church-going, hard working, nuclear African-American families, without forgetting the remaining 20%

- Stop apologizing for slavery

- Engage and employ black conservatives

These black conservatives should, using the latest statistics, consistently point out that most legislation supported by the liberals/Democrats is, in fact, inimical to the interests of the black family. Conservative talking points should have as their focus the *destructive* elements of these modern, socialist-type programs favored by neo-socialists. So Ben, are you now becoming a spokesman for the GOP and black America? In the language on the street long ago - "Not hardly." When questioned, Blacks are quite capable of speaking for themselves, but the media has apparently selected and assigned us black spokesmen almost completely without input from us. Imagine my surprise when I happened upon a major newscast and discovered the Reverends Jesse Jackson and Al Sharpton were now my official *spokespersons*.

So I suppose that leaves me, along with much of the other 80% of God-fearing, hard-working, self-supporting, tax paying African-Americans without a spokesman. The media simply lumps us all together as "Black" and has these *spokespersons* articulate our *views*. What a comfort.

Imagine the absurdity of that situation. When the media or politicians want America and the world to know what some 32 million black people are thinking, they trot out one or two "*spokespersons*" for the entire black community. Now ask these same media and political types; "Please name the official "*spokespersons*" for the white community... Bill? Hillary? Bill O'Reilly? Pat Robertson? Senator Byrd? Perhaps Dennis Kucinich or Ted Kennedy? (By the way, has anyone ever polled <u>you</u> about what <u>you</u> think?)

The fact is that Blacks have never had a national spokesperson. The closest anyone has come recently was Dr. Martin Luther King Jr., and all of us didn't agree with him. I remember his eloquent pleas for non-violence, but Malcolm, not Martin, spoke for me, and many others like me. We felt we didn't have another cheek to turn. Any sense of unanimity among Blacks had nothing to do with a national spokesman, but with the fact that "we all were catching hell." The reason so many Whites were completely surprised by the civil rights explosions of the 1960's was that *their* media anointed *black spokesmen* had been assuring them right along that *"Black folk are doin' just fine boss."*

CHAPTER 13

IT'S NOT WHAT YOU SAY...
IT'S WHAT I HEAR

ACCORDING TO MY CALCULATIONS,
THE PROBLEM DOESN'T EXIST
~ Bumper sticker

The black community, far from being monolithic, actually contains several political schools of thought and, for our purposes, two major groups with divergent perspectives. Politically, one is more active than the other and each is activated by different stimuli.

<u>Pre-'60s</u>: *That generation born prior to the '60s Civil Rights Revolution*

This more politically active group has experienced firsthand the oppressive atmosphere of institutionalized racism and they understand that while all may not be perfect, *real* change has occurred in America.

Post-'60s: *The generation born after the '60s Civil Rights Revolution*

This more vocal, more visible group may actually face a greater challenge. Subjected to a constant barrage of virtual racism propaganda by civil rights leaders, they are learning to view themselves as *victims* of the new *we are all victims of something* "*thee*-ology."

Unfortunately, for whatever reasons, most Republican initiatives focus on areas favored by the post-'60s group who generally are non-voters and stridently and vehemently anti-Republican. In a commentary published in The Black Republican magazine, Second Edition, Dr. Thomas Sowell, brilliantly outlines the failure of the Republican Party to communicate effectively with the black community:

> *"Instead of specifically targeting those black voters they might have some chance of winning, Republicans have been trying for decades to placate black "leaders," including the NAACP, and to throw Blacks such sops as stamps honoring Paul Robeson and Kwanzaa, and awarding a Medal of Freedom to Mohammad Ali. Those black voters that the Republicans have some chance of winning over are more likely to be repelled than attracted by Republicans' honoring a communist, the black separatist counterculture, and a follower of Louis Farrakhan."*

IT'S NOT WHAT YOU SAY... IT'S WHAT I HEAR

Psychiatrists, sociologists, and various and sundry counselors agree; "talk to me" is a vital ingredient in solving problems, but, the yin and yang of communication is talking *and* listening, and the art of listening is probably one of the most difficult skills to master. There have been numerous TV shows, classes, group instruction, and hundreds of books written on the subject; yet a failure to communicate still exists, even among people who have lived together for years, like husbands and wives...and Blacks and Whites.

People groups tend to communicate with each other in words or phrases that convey as much information as possible in the fewest words. Take "He's cool" for example. Loosely translated, said person, place, or thing has met the qualifications for *cool* required by the group. *Not cool/Uncool* means the standards have not been met. Affirmation by, or access to, the group is granted only when a qualified member of said group validates the applicant's credentials. "I've checked him out. He's cool." Practically every group uses some form of cultural shorthand. Evangelical Christians use *kingdom* language; drug users use street shorthand (a "fix" is not a plumbing term); hip hoppers have rap; and politicians speak poli-babble (clearly understood only by other politicians.)

In the black community, conservatives have failed to communicate their message effectively, especially to the pre '60s group, and this hampers them. Their cultural shorthand contains what I call *code words,* and these send up red flags to the pre-'60s group. Reporters, media pundits, conservatives, liberals, and both Democrats and Republicans use this code. In my opinion, the leftist and media elites use it deliberately; conservatives inadvertently, and, therefore, conservatives fail to communicate with a cultural ally ~ Blacks. Many will have the same question I had ~ "Why haven't I heard this before?"

When the northern wing of the Democrat Party was forced onto the leading edge of the Republican-supported 1964 Civil Rights Act and the 1965 Voting Rights Act, the media miraculously transformed the entire party into "liberals." When Barry Goldwater (only one of a handful of Republican senators to vote against the 1964 CRA*) became the Republican nominee for president, Republicans, by way of this same media, magically became "conservatives." In and of itself, that would not necessarily be detrimental, except for the *definition* now assigned to "conservative" by the media. Whether deliberate or not, the words "liberal" and "conservative" have been redefined and reassigned by the media. **Republicans** were the original **liberals;** **Democrats,** who ruled southern politics since 1874, were the **conservatives.** Listen carefully when you hear major media reporters and commentators (most of whom are liberal) refer to a Republican president, and his allies in Congress, as "conservatives" because coincidentally by the same media, *the most repressive, backward, anti-human rights dictator or government* will always be referred to as "conservative." However, please note; since a major voting bloc (pre-'60s white Americans) do not trust modern left leaning liberals, Democrats, no matter how far to the left, will never be referred to as *liberals* by the media.

In 1964 Democrats controlled both houses of Congress. Note the following voting record:

For passage of the 1964 Civil Rights Act:

Democrat:	Senate 60%	House 61%
Republican:	Senate 82%	House 80%

(The most critical vote was to break the filibuster in the senate to allow passage of the Civil Rights Act. Republicans voted 81% to end it, Democrats only 65%. Remember, the Democrats controlled Congress. As one wag put it, "No Republicans in Congress, no civil rights bill.")

For passage of the 1964 Voting Rights Act:

Democrat: Senate 74%   House 80%

Republican: Senate 97%   House 85%

Under President Dwight D. Eisenhower, the 1957 civil rights bill that would eventually become the 1964 Civil Rights Act was introduced to Congress. Although Senator Everett Dirksen, a Republican from Illinois, literally sacrificed his health pushing this bill through Congress and though Republicans voted overwhelmingly in favor of it, it was the predominantly anti-civil rights Democrat-controlled Congress that was congratulated by the press. It is difficult to believe this was purely accidental coming from a press corps that by its own admission is "overwhelmingly liberal" and "consistently votes Democrat" according to an eye-opening study of the media elites.

Here are a few key findings from this major study conducted by Professors S. Robert Lichter and Stanley Rothman:

- Eighty-one percent of the journalists interviewed voted for the Democratic presidential candidate in every election between 1964 and 1976.

- In the Democratic landslide of 1964, ninety-four percent of the press surveyed voted for President Lyndon Johnson (D) over Senator Barry Goldwater (R).

- In 1968, eighty percent of the press surveyed voted for Democrat Senator Hubert Humphrey.

- In 1972, when sixty-two percent of the electorate chose President Richard Nixon, eighty-one percent of the media elite voted for liberal Democratic Senator George McGovern.

- In 1976, the Democratic nominee, Jimmy Carter, won eighty-one percent of the reporters surveyed. Nineteen percent chose Gerald Ford.

- Over the 16-year period of the study, the Republican candidate always received less than twenty percent of the media elite's vote.

Furthermore,

- Lichter and Rothman's survey of journalists discovered that "Fifty-four percent placed themselves to the left of center, compared to only nineteen percent who chose the right side of the spectrum."

- "Fifty-six percent said the people they worked with were mostly on the left, and only eight percent on the right — a margin of seven-to-one." [25]

So much for unbiased reporting from the major "drive-by media."

This redefining of the key words *liberal* and *conservative* by the media is especially unfortunate for Republicans, because one word conveys a totally different message to another primary voting group, pre-'60s African-Americans.

To most Americans (especially white Christian Republicans), *conservative* means:

- **Local control** = self-determination
- **State's rights** = individual liberties
- **Smaller, non-interventionist federal government** = strong national defense and lower taxes
- **Strict constructionist judiciary** = constitutionally accurate judges

Good solid conservative values all, but words mean different things to different people so, it's not what you say...it's what I hear that matters.

The pre-'60s African-Americans have an entirely different perspective; the *"conservatives"* in their generation supported segregation with those **exact same words**.

Conservative was, and for many white supremacists still is, *code* for:

- **Local control** = KKK, white citizens councils, Jim Crow (segregated schools, restrooms, water fountains, etc.) ~ i.e., southern racists controlling every aspect of black existence

- **State's rights** = "Segregation now and forever!" The Civil War was fought over the state's right to retain its black citizens in slavery. The federal government was to have no jurisdiction over state's affairs.

- **Smaller non-interventionist federal government** = the federal government will not intervene on behalf of its black citizens. No Constitutional guarantees of citizenship

- **Strict constructionist Judiciary** = Judicial support for local governments; a conservative angle to the Constitution. Conservative judges would interpret the Constitution to mean "no federal intervention" in local affairs, particularly as regards race.

Therefore, when pre-'60s African-Americans hear *conservative* they still hear *Lynchings...Night Riders...Voter Suppression...Police Dogs...Fire Hoses...Segregation.* However, since Republicans have been relabeled "conservatives," the post-'60s group sees them as the enemy. Democrats have become the *liberals* and are now "friends of the family." What has been forgotten, deliberately obscured, or lost in translation is the fact that the **pre-'60s conservatives using those code words were all Democrats.** Accordingly, many African-Americans in both the pre and post-'60s groups who espouse conservative values vote Democrat in a mistaken devotion to a perceived, but undocumented, history of support by Democrats for the civil rights of Blacks. Lynching was a fact; segregation was a fact; prejudice, injustice, and discrimination are facts. While it has been all the rage to blame Whites in general, the Democrat Party (the original conservatives) which owes much of its early political successes to the KKK, is ultimately responsible for short-circuiting almost all of the economic and social progress that would have accrued to black Americans.

Okay. Got it! *Republicans were the original liberals and Democrats were the original conservatives.*

BLACK TO THE FUTURE

In the decades since Reconstruction, African-Americans have made almost unimaginable strides, despite specifically targeted barriers and intense local, state, and even some national hostility. Would any reasonable person attempt to argue, objectively, that America has not progressed, literally by leaps and bounds, both socially and economically since the 1964 Civil Rights Act? In their book, *America in Black and White; One Nation, Indivisible,* co-authors Abigail and Stephan Thernstrom pointed out; *"No group in American history has ever improved its position so dramatically in so short a time."*

One can only begin to imagine the impact on the overall political, cultural, and economic life of the United States had a Democrat president not ordered the removal of 40,000 freed slaves from 400,000 acres of prime land. Can you visualize what America would be like today had not a Democrat-controlled Congress reversed the anti-segregation provisions of the civil rights legislation passed by Republicans in 1866, 1870, 1871, and 1875? The impact on the world, not just America, of millions of free Blacks having lived and worked for 200 years in a colorblind society would be incalculable. Literally trillions more dollars would have been generated by the American economy, making the most robust economic engine ever to exist even more powerful.

TALK TO THE PEOPLE THE PEOPLE LISTEN TO

Few Blacks subscribe to the "separation of church and state" doctrine. This is one reason Democrats add the obligatory church stop (complete with sermons and campaign contributions) to all campaign stops. This will be one of the few times they visit the black community and, interestingly, the liberal media will discover no "violation of church and state." (Just try *that* as a Republican).

Unquestionably, one of, if not the most influential institutions in the African-American community is still the church.

Bishops who have been elected to head their denominations and pastors, who by popular acclaim through support of their message oversee mega churches, wield an enormous amount of influence among Blacks, especially the pre-'60s generation. Since Reconstruction, the Black church has served as a source of strength, comfort, and leadership. Ministers in the black community are, for the most part, accorded respect and a majority of leaders in that community bear the title "Reverend" before their names, a condition not existing in the white community to a similar degree.

An honest dialogue between the true leaders of the African-American community and the true leaders of our republic is one of the solutions to the *Black Yellow Dog* trend in the black community. I don't mean monologues by media elites and ideologues, rap sessions on college campuses, or high-sounding rhetoric from neo-liberal think tanks, but open communication where both sides *listen*.

CHAPTER 14

"WE, THE PEOPLE" ~ YOU AND ME!

THINGS THAT MAKE YOU GO "HHMMMM"
~ Arsenio Hall

R ace is a wholly arbitrary classification, based on political, economic, and governmental considerations; it has no true scientific basis.

In early Colonial times, *Christians* or *Englishmen* were the official classifications, no*t race.*

A census is required by the Constitution every 10 years; at the first census (1790) the issue was primarily who was slave or free. (Again, the Three-Fifths Clause was about numbers, not race.)

"The difference between the right word and <u>almost</u> the right word is the difference between lightning and a lightning bug."
~ Mark Twain

"So what do I say to Colored, Negro, Black, Afro-American, er, ahem, ummmm — you people?"

~ White Questioner

VIRGINIA LAWS DEFINING *COLOREDS*: [1]

1705:   Any "child, grandchild, or great grandchild of a Negro" (Mulatto)

1866:   Every person having one-fourth or more Negro blood shall be deemed a Colored person. (Quadroon)

1910:   Any person with 1/16th blood is black. (Octoroon)

1924:   The Virginia Racial Purity Act - "the one-drop" rule defines as Black, Negro, Colored any person having one drop of black blood.

Just a thought ~ wonder which political party controlled Virginia politics from 1878 for almost 100 years? (Here's a hint: Dem...)

Proving somebody has 1/16 black blood, much less one drop, might be difficult. In some cases, depending on your physical appearance and whether or not you felt compelled to *fess up,* you could cross a state line and change races, literally. Many Octoroons and "one droppers" simply moved north and passed as white the rest of their lives. All of which brings us back to the original question - how do you define race? *A wholly arbitrary classification based on political, economic, and governmental considerations, without scientific underpinnings.*

Since it is immediately recognizable, the most common determination of race is generally skin color. Technically, a true "white" person would be an *albino*, one who is deficient in the substance that colors the skin, melanin. There are Black albinos. Or is that a "white-*Black* albino?" Or a "Black-*white* albino?" And is a Black albino a White? According to the Human Genome Project, the human body produces melanin in a variety of colors ~ shades of brown, yellow, and red (pure melanin is the color of charcoal dust) ~ and scientists have determined that our skin color is determined by a substance that comprises no more than 0.01% of our estimated 35,000 genes. Harold Freeman, Director of the National Cancer Institute's Center to Reduce Health Disparities, said: *"Race disappears when you look at the human genome."* A geneticist at U.C. Berkeley, Dr. Sylvia Spengler, is convinced that *"... Given what we know about human genetics...the tall person and the short person are significantly more different than the black man and the white man."*

Aha!! Now *that* makes sense; short people are clearly inferior, easily identifiable, and cannot pass as tall, no matter the blood drop count. It is obvious to me; racial classification should be according to height, not color. Moreover, for Affirmative Action proponents, short people could obviously use a *head* start. Speaking of head starts, why not expand the boundaries of Affirmative Action? In the spirit of fair play, let's give Whites a head start in the 100-meter dash, and on the basketball court compel Blacks to guard only other Blacks, because everybody knows "white men can't jump."

AMERICA THE BEAUTIFUL

Recently, it has become trendy to disparage and malign the American dream and criticize the lady with the torch of freedom held high. To me it seems strange that nearly all the calumny comes from those fortunate enough to live in the glow of that torch.

"Give me your tired, your poor,

Your huddled masses yearning to breathe free,

The wretched refuse of your teeming shore.

Send these, the homeless, tempest-tossed to me,

I lift my lamp beside the golden door."

These words from the inscription on the base of the Statue of Liberty are not merely a few meaningless high-sounding empty phrases; they declare the power and purpose of the American dream. The world's "wretched, homeless, tempest tossed, yearning to be free" continually risk all for the slightest chance to walk these blessed shores. There are no inherent restrictions on the progress of citizens of the United States and there is abundant evidence of the ability of individuals to rise above the circumstances of their birth, background, race, gender, or national origin. The real strength of the American experiment is in the power to change what you were.

WHAT IS THAT IN THINE HAND?
~ *Exodus 4:1-2*

The following anecdote has been reported as occurring in a variety of ways. My favorite version is found in an excellent book written by Michael Novak, *On Two Wings: Humble Faith and Common Sense at the American Founding* —

At the banquet soon after to celebrate the conclusion of the Constitutional Convention of 1787, a Philadelphia matron rushed toward its most senior delegate; *"Oh! Mr. Franklin,"* she gushed. *"What have you gentlemen wrought after so many weeks of secrecy behind those thick doors?"* Franklin is said to have adjusted his glasses before offering his famous retort: *"A republic, Madam, if you can keep it."*

"A republic..." ~ "We, the People"

The future of the American republic does not lie in the hands of some rogue dictator nor hostile army gathered on some distant shore. The danger lies not without, but within. A republic requires elected representatives who carry out the will of an informed electorate who have made intelligent decisions regarding their future. The right to vote, the power to participate in those decisions that will affect one's life, is a right guaranteed by the Constitution to every American citizen.

"... if you can keep it." We recall the words of John Adams:

"We have no government armed with power capable of contending with human passions unbridled by morality and religion...our Constitution was made only for a moral and religious people. It is wholly inadequate to the government of any other."

Perhaps the writings of a Scottish historian, Sir A. F. Tytler, influenced George Washington, James Madison, John Adams, and other Founding Fathers as they contemplated a form of government for this fledgling new country. What form of government would best serve a "religious and moral" people? A constitutional monarchy? They were aware of the shortcoming of kings and tyrants, had suffered greatly under a monarchy, and knew well how quickly a monarch could abolish a constitution.

A democracy? Tytler, their contemporary, had this warning:

"A democracy....can only exist until the voters discover they can vote themselves largesse from the public treasury." From that moment on, the majority always votes for the candidate promising the most benefits ... with the result that a democracy always collapses over loose fiscal policy, always followed by a dictatorship."

Not a monarchy! Not a democracy! In the words of Madison's Federalist Nr. 14, this would be something *"new and more noble...*[a] *revolution which has no parallel in the annals of human society...the fabrics of governments which have no model on the face of the globe...the design of a great Confederacy, which it is incumbent on their successors to improve and perpetuate."* [2]

Their successors? *"We, The People..."* ~ You and Me. It is our continuing responsibility, our challenge, to improve and perpetuate this "great Confederacy" ~ the United States of America. "We, the People..." must ensure our elected representatives are not hearing exclusively the siren call of special interest groups, and we have an even more solemn duty to ensure that we, the people, do not become the special interest groups demanding "largesse from the public treasury."

Tytler had an even more sober word of warning:

"The average age of the world's great civilizations has been 200 years. These nations have progressed through this sequence...

From bondage to spiritual faith;

From spiritual faith to great courage;

From courage to liberty;

From liberty to abundance;

From abundance to selfishness;

From selfishness to complacency;

From complacency to apathy;

From apathy to dependency;

From dependency back to bondage"

To Americans of every political persuasion, culture, gender, and ethnicity, I address these questions: At 400 years, where are we on that timeline? The Founding Fathers entrusted the future to us. To whom have we entrusted our future? As America has just celebrated her 400th birthday, will our children's children be able to celebrate a half millennium of liberty?

I am confidently optimistic they will. I have an abundance of hope for the future and an unshakeable faith in God and the wisdom of all Americans. I take comfort in the knowledge that somewhere, somehow African-Americans will hear the truth *and the truth shall make us free.*

To this end, I write.

EPILOGUE

"Never discuss religion or politics," we are admonished. While there may be a degree of truth there, the truth is, one's faith, or lack thereof, will always determine one's politics; but then, maybe not.

"Integrity" can be defined as saying and doing the same thing; "hypocrisy" as saying one thing but doing another. Is "hypocrite" too strong a word for persons of faith who fail to vote their faith? Arguably one of the most religious groups in America, Blacks often find themselves in the unenviable position of voting against their own religious beliefs. They generally oppose same-sex marriages and abortions but, by voting as Yellow Dog Democrats, actually find themselves helping to elect candidates who openly support the very issues they oppose.

Faith can be defined as the unquestioning acceptance of a person, place, or thing without substantive evidence. *Blind* is defined as being without the ability to see. *Blind faith* could thus be defined as the unquestioning acceptance of a thing without seeing any concrete proof; in other words, accepting something as true with no absolute proof of its validity. Outside the realm of an authentic religious experience, reason cautions against unverified acceptance of any claim, regardless of its origin. The God of the Judeo-Christian Bible does not demand or require blind faith; He left abundant proof of His existence. He requires only an objective examination of the evidence to reach an intelligent conclusion based upon one's own research. Should a greater measure of trust be accorded something as demonstrably untrustworthy as a political party? If the Almighty does not require blind faith, should a politician? If the Creator of the universe provides reasonable and logical support for believing in Him, is it an intelligent decision to believe politicians without some tangible evidence of the validity of their claims?

The Founding Fathers, who were mostly Christians (some Deists), were keenly aware of the nature of man. John Adams, second President of the United States, cut right to the chase:

"We have no government armed with power capable of contending with human passions unbridled by morality and religion...our Constitution was made only for a moral and religious people. It is wholly inadequate to the government of any other."

His comments echoed this earlier observation attributed to the first President, George Washington: *"It is impossible to rightly govern a nation without God and the Bible."* Patrick Henry, best known for his "liberty or death" speech declared, *"Virtue, morality, and religion. This is the armor, my friend, and this alone that renders us invincible..."* [1]

At this point, the specious argument, "The *Constitution* mandates the separation of church and state!" will invariably be raised. That oft-cited phrase does actually exist. It is found in Article 52 of the Constitution: *"The church in the USSR is separated from the state, and the school from the church."* That is *not* a misprint. The doctrine of the "separation of church and state," so assiduously supported by organizations like People for the American Way, Americans United for Separation of Church and State, the ACLU, and other leftist and atheist organizations, is taken almost verbatim from the Constitution of the old Union of Soviet Socialist Republics (the USSR), ratified in 1977 under Leonid Brezhnev.[2]

The ubiquitous phrase "separation of church and state" exists *nowhere in any of our founding documents* - not the U.S. Constitution, not the Declaration of Independence, nor any other document pertaining to the establishment and maintenance of the American republic. That the framers of our liberties had no such nonsense in mind is evidenced by this statement from Benjamin Franklin in an address to the Constitutional Convention in 1787: *"I have lived, a long time, and the longer I live, the more convincing proofs I see of this truth — that God Governs in the affairs of men. And if a sparrow cannot fall to the ground without His notice, is it probable that an empire can rise without His aid?"*

The phrase, "separation of church and state," taken out of context, eagerly seized upon, and used as the basis for dismantling the 1st Amendment comes from a letter written by then President Thomas Jefferson in reply to a group of Baptist ministers in Danbury, Connecticut. The ministers had written to Jefferson regarding their concerns that *"the right to worship be not as a result of favors granted, but as the inalienable right of free men."*

THE ADDRESS OF THE DANBURY BAPTIST ASSOCIATION, IN THE STATE OF CONNECTICUT; ASSEMBLED OCTOBER 7TH 1801.

To Thomas Jefferson Esq., the President of the United States of America.

Sir,

"... Our sentiments are uniformly on the side of religious liberty—that religion is at all times and places a matter between God and individuals—that no man ought to suffer in name, person, or effects on account of his religious opinions—that the legitimate power of civil government extends no further than to punish the man who works ill to his neighbors... religion is considered as the first object of legislation; and therefore what religious privileges we enjoy (as a minor part of the state) we enjoy as favors granted, and not as inalienable rights; and these favors ...are inconsistent with the rights of freemen. It is not to be wondered at therefore; if those who seek after power and gain under the pretense of government and religion should reproach their fellow men... as a enemy of religion, law, and good order, because he will not, dare not, assume the prerogatives of Jehovah and make laws to govern the kingdom of Christ..."

"A Committee of the Danbury Baptist Association, in the State of Connecticut."

~~~~~~~~~

Jefferson's reply:

Messrs. Nehemiah Dodge, Ephraim Robbins, and Stephen S. Nelson

Washington, January 1, 1802

Gentlemen, The affectionate sentiment of esteem and approbation which you are so good as to express towards me, on behalf of the Danbury Baptist Association, give me the highest satisfaction. My duties dictate a faithful and zealous pursuit of the interests of my constituents, and in proportion as they are persuaded of my fidelity to those duties, the discharge of them becomes more and more pleasing. Believing with you that religion is a matter which lies solely between man and his God, that he owes account to none other for his faith or his worship, that the legislative powers of government reach actions only, and not opinions, <u>I contemplate with sovereign reverence that act of the whole American people which declared that their legislature would make no law respecting an establishment of religion, or prohibiting the free exercise thereof, thus building a wall of separation between Church and State</u>. Adhering to this expression of the supreme will of the nation in behalf of the rights of conscience, I shall see with sincere satisfaction the progress of those sentiments which tend to restore to man all his natural rights, convinced he has no natural right in opposition to his social duties.(Emphasis Added).

I reciprocate your kind prayers for the protection and blessing of the common Father and Creator of man, and tender you for yourselves and your religious association, assurances of my high respect and esteem."

Th. Jefferson, Jan.1.1802. [3]

The Framers had neither the notion nor the slightest intention of separating their faith and their politics. When communicating with the Danbury Baptists, Jefferson wrote of a wall *protecting*, not *separating*, religion from government. Read objectively and in context, his letter leaves little doubt; he was assuring the Baptist ministers that any "wall of separation" was there to restrain the *government - not the governed*.

The language of the 1st Amendment is quite specific: "*Congress* (not local school boards, city councils, judges, or the Supreme Court) *shall make no law respecting an establishment of* [a specific] *religion, nor prohibiting the free exercise thereof.*" Sans lawyer, I reviewed this short, specific address regarding religion and the power to control it, and one thing seems bothersome. When leftist judges and misguided public officials forbid people to practice their faith under the "establishment clause," does that not immediately and specifically violate the Free Exercise Clause? It seems to me that the United States Constitution says "Congress, do not make any laws establishing or interfering with our free exercise of religion; leave it alone – we, the people, will decide!" (emphasis added)

The men intimately involved in the founding of the United States of America were convinced that an acknowledgement of the Creator was inextricably bound up in the life of the nation. The Founding Fathers were not deceived regarding the inherent dangers of a secular society. This has been nowhere more clearly stated than in a statement often attributed to John Quincy Adams, sixth President of the United States: "*The highest glory of the American Revolution was this; it connected in one indissoluble bond the principles of civil government with those of Christianity.*" This "indissoluble bond" between the Founders' faith and their politics (which liberal, irreligious, activist America haters are working ever harder to destroy), is the basis for our liberties as a nation and the foundation of this powerful engine of human liberty. John Witherspoon, a signer of the Declaration of Independence, a leader in the Continental Congress, and the sixth president of Princeton University, held another view of this type of activism; *"Whoever is an avowed enemy of God, I scruple not to call him an enemy to his country."* [4]

Lately there has been a great deal of criticism of the ideas inherited from "a bunch of dead old white guys," (aka the Founding Fathers) but what other nation in all of history has America's overall record of progress in human and civil rights? By all means, include slavery, but also include the deaths of tens of thousands of young men in a civil war to abolish it, and billions of dollars, plus continuing legislation to expunge its legacy.

America is the most powerful, most stable, longest-lasting form of government (a republic - not a democracy) ever to exist, period. It is also the wealthiest. Over two billion people worldwide earn less than $1,000 year. Eighty-five percent of the world's population (with families averaging from three to seven children), earn less than $8,000 a year. In the United States, a family of *one* (at this writing) would be in "poverty" at $10,210 ($11,750 in Hawaii, and $12,770 in Alaska). Poverty in America is the equivalent of middle to upper middle class in most of the world.[5]

America, as of yet, is not and was never intended to be a secular society – for good reason. Ultimately, a secular society, as demonstrated by countries like China, the now defunct USSR, and some of its former satellites can maintain public order only through coercion. People who support a purely secular position must of necessity support ever-increasing government activity, intervention, and legislation to manage public behavior. George Washington underscored this in his final farewell address to the nation; an admonition so stirring that Jefferson established it as required reading at the University of Virginia:

> *"Of all the dispositions and habits which lead to political pros-*
> *perity, religion and morality are indispensable supports. In*
> *vain would that man claim the tribute of patriotism who*
> *should labor to subvert these great pillars of human happiness*
> *— these firmest props of the duties of men and citizens.*
>
> *The mere politician, equally with the pious man, ought to*
> *respect and to cherish them. A volume could not trace all their*
> *connections with private and public felicity. Let it simply be*
> *asked, Where is the security for property, for reputation, for*
> *life, if the sense of religious obligation desert the oaths which*
> *are the instruments of investigation in courts of justice?*
>
> *And let us with caution indulge the supposition that morality*
> *can be maintained without religion. Whatever may be con-*
> *ceded to the influence of refined education on minds of pecu-*
> *liar structure, reason and experience both forbid us to expect*
> *that national morality can prevail in exclusion of religious*
> *principle."*

Let us today, with extreme caution, indulge that same sup-position *"… that national morality can prevail in exclusion of reli-gious principle."*

At the risk of stepping into a politically incorrect mine field, the fact of the matter is, the Founders of the American Republic were obviously and specifically referring to the religion of the

Judeo-Christian Bible. The political, religious, and personal free-doms (including the right of dissent) enjoyed, and unfortunate-ly taken for granted by Western civilization in general and America in particular, is a derivative of the Judeo-Christian worldview and can only exist freely in societies founded upon this worldview. *"It is when a people forget God that tyrants forge their chains. A vitiated "weakened or debased" state of morals, a corrupted public conscience, is incompatible with freedom."* (Patrick Henry)

History and an unbiased view of the geopolitical world of today verify this.

The genesis of political parties may have been altruism, but today, for all practical intents and purposes, most political functionaries are more concerned with concealing their true motives - re-election at all costs - than with serving their constituency.

A French historian and political scientist, Alexis de Tocqueville visited America in the 1800s and was deeply impressed with the people's commitment to God and country. According to published reports, he said:

> *"I sought for the greatness and genius of America in her commodious harbors and her ample rivers—and it was not there ... in her fertile fields and boundless forests—and it was not there ... in her rich mines and her vast world commerce—and it was not there ... in her democratic Congress and her matchless Constitution—and it was not there. Not until I went into the churches of America and heard her pulpits flame with righteousness did I understand the secret of her genius and power. America is great because she is good, and if America ever ceases to be good, America will cease to be great."* [6]

The Founding Fathers were not perfect, but they knew right from wrong, good from evil, and made the best decisions possible given the harsh realities of the day. They believed the future of America rested upon the character, integrity, and continued moral growth of a Bible reading people. *Because* of their faith, they understood that the continued existence of a free republic depended upon moral virtues exercised from within, by individuals who understand that a society of individuals is held together *as a whole*, not by externally imposed law, but by internally imposed self government. It is therefore no accident; the most prominent words in one of the most profound documents ever made by man, the Constitution of the United States of America, are *"We, The People."*

Some two hundred thirty years ago, the phrase *"We, the People"* excluded some of the people. To secure the rights of *all* the people, we have had major amendments to our Constitution, a Civil War, nine civil rights acts, a voting rights act, and numerous U.S. Supreme Court decisions.

As we celebrate four hundred years of the founding of America, this great republic has in place, and is actively pursuing and diligently implementing, the elements necessary to make the dream of millions a reality, as articulated by Nobel Laureate Martin Luther King Jr.

Yellow Dog Democrats, *Conservatives*, and *Liberals* have become an integral part of the American lexicon, as have the words of Dr. King to the tens of thousands gathered at the Lincoln Memorial on August 28, 1963:

> ...*"I say to you today my friends...even though we face the difficulties of today and tomorrow, I still have a dream. It is a dream deeply rooted in the American dream.*

I have a dream that one day this nation will rise up and live out the true meaning of its creed: "We hold these truths to be self-evident: that all men are created equal."

I have a dream that one day on the red hills of Georgia the sons of former slaves and the sons of former slave owners will be able to sit down together at the table of brotherhood.

I have a dream that one day even the state of Mississippi, a state sweltering with the heat of injustice, sweltering with the heat of oppression, will be transformed into an oasis of freedom and justice.

I have a dream that my four little children will one day live in a nation where they will not be judged by the color of their skin but by the content of their character.

I have a dream today.

I have a dream that one day, down in Alabama, with its vicious racists, with its governor having his lips dripping with the words of interposition and nullification; one day right there in Alabama, little black boys and black girls will be able to join hands with little white boys and white girls as sisters and brothers.

I have a dream today.

When we allow freedom to ring, when we let it ring from every village and every hamlet, from every state and every city, we will be able to speed up that day when all of God's children, black men and white men, Jews and Gentiles, Protestants and Catholics, will be able to join hands and sing in the words of the old Negro spiritual, "Free at last! Free at last! Thank God Almighty, we are free at last!"

NOTES

INTRODUCTION

1. "http://www.pbs.org/newshour/bb/law/july-dec98/thomas_7-29.html"

CHAPTER 1

1. "http://www.fee.org/publications/the-freeman/article.asp?aid=2498"

2. "http://www.virtualjamestown.org/timeline2.html"

3. "http://www.dinsdoc.com/russell-1.htm" (Original MS. Records of the County Court of Northampton. Orders, Deeds and Wills, 1651-1654, p. 10.)

4. "http://www.dinsdoc.com/russell-1.htm" (MS. Deeds of Henrico County, No. 5, p. 585.)

5. "http://mshistory.k12.ms.us/features/feature4/freeblacks.html"

6. "http://mshistory.k12.ms.us/features/feature36/forks_of_the_road.html"

CHAPTER 2

1. "http://www.bartleby.com/100/245.21.html"

2. "http://hnn.us/roundup/entries/12782.html"

3. "http://hnn.us/roundup/entries/12782.html" Ibid.

4. "http://www.loc.gov/exhibits/treasures/trt001.html"

5. "http://www.shadowconventions.com/losangeles/index.html"

6. <u>A House Divided, America in the Age of Lincoln</u>, Foner & Mahoney

7. "http://www.wallbuilders.com/resources/search/detail.php?ResourceID=34" (*The Records of the Federal Convention of 1787*, Max Farrand, editor (New Haven: Yale University Press, 1911), Vol. I, p. 201.)

8. "http://www.wallbuilders.com/resources/search/detail.php?ResourceID=34" (James Madison, *The Debates in the Federal Convention of 1787*

Which Framed the Constitution of the United States of America, Gaillart Hint and James Brown Scott, editors (New York: Oxford University Press, 1920), p. 239.)

9. "http://www.online-literature.com/frederick_douglass/bondage_freedom/25/"

10. "http://american_almanac.tripod.com/fredlinc.htm"

11. "http://www.wallbuilders.com/resources/search/detail.php?ResourceID=11" (Thomas Jefferson, *Notes on the State of Virginia* (New York: M. L. & W. A. Davis, 1794, Second Edition), pp. 240-242, Query XVIII.

12. "http://www.wallbuilders.com/resources/search/detail.php?ResourceID=11" (*Journals of the Continental Congress,* Volume XXVI, pp. 118-119, Monday, March 1, 1784.

13. "http://www.wallbuilders.com/resources/search/detail.php?ResourceID=11" (*The Revised Code of the Laws of Virginia: Being A Collection of all Such Acts of the General Assembly, of a Public and Permanent Nature, as are Now in Force* (Richmond: Printed by Thomas Ritcher, 1819), pp. 433-436.)

CHAPTER 3

1. "http://www.vlib.us/amdocs/texts/kansas.html"

CHAPTER 4

1. "http://www.law.cornell.edu/supct/html/historics/USSC_CR_0060_0393_ZO.html"

2. "http://usinfo.state.gov/usa/infousa/facts/democrac/21.htm"

3. "http://www.archives.gov/exhibits/featured_documents/emancipation_proclamation/transcript.html"

4. "http://www.civilwarhome.com/lincolngreeley.htm"

CHAPTER 5

1. "http://www.civil-war.net/cw_images/files/images/309.jpg"

2. "http://www.civilwarhome.com/Battles.htm"

3. "http://www.civilwarhome.com/casualties.htm"

4. Clipping from New-York Daily Tribune, [13 Feb. 1865], "Negroes of Savannah," Consolidated Correspondence File, ser. 225, Central Records, Quartermaster General, Record Group 92, National Archives.

5. By order of Major General W.T. Sherman:, No. 15., Headquarters Military Division of the Mississippi, 16 Jan. 1865, Orders & Circulars, Ser. 44, Adjutant General's Office, Record Group, 9

CHAPTER 7

1. "http://www.wallbuilders.com"

2. "http://www.wallbuilders.com/resources/search/detail.php?ResourceID=34" (Edward A. Johnson, *A School History of the Negro Race in American from 1619 to 1890* (Raleigh: Edwards & Broughton, 1891), p. 170.

3. "http://www.wallbuilders.com/resources/search/detail.php?ResourceID=34" (African Methodist Episcopal Church Review (Ohio: Theophilus J. Minton) April, 1892, Vol. VIII, No. IV, p. 369, from an Article on Robert Brown Elliot.
    [http://dbs.ohiohistory.org/africanam/det.cfm?ID2373]

4. Ibid. p. 364.

5. "http://history.furman.edu/~benson/hst41/blue/stevens1.htm"

6. "http://www.yale.edu/ynhti/curriculum/units/1979/2/79.02.04.x.html"

CHAPTER 8

1. "http://www.answers.com/topic/compromise-of-1877"

2. "http://www.oyez.org/cases/1851-1900/1895/1895_210/"

3. "http://www.oyez.org/cases/1851-1900/1895/1895_210/" Ibid.

CHAPTER 9

1. "http://www.mediaresearch.org/biasbasics/biasbasics3.asp"

2. "http://www.wallbuilders.com/resources/search/detail.php?ResourceID=63" (House of Representatives Mis. Doc. No. 53, "Condition of

Affairs in Mississippi" Evidence Taken By The Committee on Reconstruction, 40th Congress, 3rd Session, December 15, 1868.)

3. Taking Jim Crow out of Uniform: A. Philip Randolph and the desegregation of the U.S. military - Special Report: The Integrated Military - 50
Years - COPYRIGHT 1997 Cox, Matthews & Associates /COPYRIGHT
2004 Gale Group

CHAPTER 10

1. "http://www.wallbuilders.com/resources/search/detail.php?Resour-
ceID=34"

2. "http://www.wallbuilders.com"

CHAPTER 11

1. "http://www.gmu.edu/departments/economics/wew/articles/02/
standards.html"

2. "http://www.nationalreview.com/levin/levin122002.asp"

3. Melba Pattillo Beals, Warriors Don't Cry: A Searing Memoir of the Battle
to Integrate Little Rock's Central High (New York: Washington Square
Press, 1994

CHAPTER 12

1. "http://www.washingtoninformer.com/ARAffirmativeActionHero
2005July21.html"

2. Washington Post/Kaiser Family Foundation/Harvard University/Racial Atti-
tude Survey 2001: Black Pride and Black Prejudice: Snyderman and Piazza

CHAPTER 14

1. "http://www.pbs.org/race/000_About/002_03_c-godeeper.htm"

2. "http://en.wikisource.org/wiki/The_Federalist_Papers/No._14"

EPILOGUE

1. "http://quotes.liberty-tree.ca/quote/patrick_henry_quote_7127"

2. "http://www.constitution.org/cons/ussr77.txt"

3. Source: Thomas Jefferson, The Writings of Thomas Jefferson, Albert E. Bergh, ed. (Washington, D. C.: The Thomas Jefferson Memorial Association of the United States, 1904), Vol. XVI, pp. 281-282

4. "http://quotes.liberty-tree.ca/quote/john_witherspoon_quote_53b6"

5. Gallup International polls of ideal family size; the Guttmacher Institute family values studies; papers to the 2004 World Congress on Bioethics; Johns Hopkins INFO project reports; papers to the 2001 World Population Conference; the European Foundation qquality of life studies; UN Population Prospects 2004 Revision report.

6. "http://www.bibleweb.com/2006/12/de-tocqueville-america-is-great-because.htm"

Printed in the United States
202897BV00002B/112-156/P

9 781600 372841